A Legacy of Opium

The true story of how three brothers from Tenby
became opium traders in China,
and of their legacy.

by **Douglas Fraser**

Published by Tenby Heritage Publications
Tenby Museum and Art Gallery
Castle Hill
Tenby
Pembrokeshire SA70 7BP

a joint venture of Tenby Museum and Art Gallery, and Tenby Historical Society.

ISBN: 978-0-9565396-0-1

Contents

Tenby from Castle Hill 1821 – Charles Norris (1779 – 1858)
Tenby Museum and Art Gallery

Introduction

Those of us who are fortunate enough to own an an old and interesting house usually enjoy researching its history. Yet when researching the history of Tenby's Lexden Terrace, I did not expect to stumble across a story of piracy and smuggling in the South China seas, a story of opium trading, a story which had been lost, possibly deliberately hidden, for over 150 years.

That is the story related in the following pages. It describes how three brothers from Tenby, sons of a local seaman, went to China to make their fortunes. How John Rees, the most successful, went on to become a major landowner in Pembrokeshire and how his family became part of the progressive political establishment in Hampstead. Finally, how the whole tale was quietly forgotten in the light of our Victorian ancestors' justified disgust with the opium trade.

There are many consequences which have arisen from the opium trade, including lives blighted and the distrust which still exists between China and the West, China's "Century of Shame". This account is of smaller but fortunately more benign legacies. Some are tangible such as the houses that John Rees built for himself and his bride, houses still standing in Tenby. Some are intangible, such as the significant contributions to social welfare made by his family, contributions that were only made possible because of the position in society that they had gained from the proceeds of the opium trade.

Douglas Fraser
May 2010.

Tenby Museum and Art Gallery
Castle Hill
Tenby,
Pembrokeshire SA70 7BP
01834 842 809
www.tenbymuseum.org.uk

Tenby Museum is the oldest independent museum in Wales.

Tenby Historical Society

Tenby Historical Society organises talks and visits, and seeks to promote support for and understanding of Tenby's heritage.

Tenby Harbour from the North by Charles Norris. About 1830. Tenby Museum and Art Gallery.

Chapter 1 The Rees Family of Tenby

Tenby, *Dinbych-y-Pysgod* in Welsh, is a walled, mediaeval trading and fishing port in Pembrokeshire, in the south west corner of Wales. Prosperous in the middle ages, by the end of the eighteenth century its once fine houses were crumbling and pigs roamed the streets. After preaching in Tenby in 1784, John Wesley, the founder of the Methodist Church, said *"Two thirds of the ancient town are either in ruins or vanished away"*. Yet Wesley also praised the beauty of Tenby's setting and others shared his opinions since it was about then that Tenby started to develop as a fashionable seaside resort.

Of course only the wealthy could enjoy Tenby for recreation. The fastest means of travel from England involved a trip of eighteen hours by sailing boat from Bristol and hence the Town could enjoy the sense of remoteness and exclusivity which is now associated with exotic holiday locations. Two sons of the Earl of Warwick, Charles and Robert Fulke Greville, built holiday homes in St Julian Street before 1800. Sir William Paxton who had made a fortune in India, commenced a programme of development in 1805 which included a fine bath house. *Merroney 2004, Tipton 1987.*

Tenby High Street about 1820 by Charles Norris. Tenby Museum and Art Gallery.

During the first decades of the nineteenth century the most tumbledown houses, such as the mansion of the once prominent White family (above) were pulled down. Old houses were refaced in the fashionable Georgian style - many apparently Georgian or Victorian houses in the Town today have mediaeval cores. New terraces were built in St Julian Street which winds down through the town to the Harbour, and on the Croft and the Norton on the outskirts of the Town. By 1843, Mary Anne Bourne in what was admittedly a holiday guide, could say *"The natural beauty of Tenby, its romantic situation and scenery together with its eligible position and obvious advantages as a bathing place caught the eye of taste and wealth...It has been for nearly 50 years the favourite summer resort of rank and fashion."*

The Reinagle print which follows shows the Greville houses – with curved facades – from Castle Beach. The site adjoining them, on the right hand side and edged by a row of single storey cottages, belonged to Green Gardens, a fine old house just out of sight. In 1843 Green Gardens was pulled down and work started on Lexden Terrace.

Merroney 2004, Tipton 1987.

Print by G P Reinagle from about 1830; Pembrokeshire County Library.

Lexden Terrace comprises six houses in a full Regency style, described by Pevsner (The Buildings of Pembrokeshire) as *"Tenby's finest C19th work"*. They face St Julian Street but the backs of the houses overlook Castle Beach and the sea. The first five houses were built by John Smith, for a Captain John Rees. John Smith is a well documented Tenby builder of the period but, until the research was carried out which led to this account, John Rees was a shadowy figure. Even the thoroughly researched Pevsner described him in 2004 as a *"developer and speculator"*, not because of evidence but presumably because of a lack of any alternative explanation.

So who was John Rees and why did he have such a low profile? We know from the 1851 census return for Tenby that he was born in the Town but in the 1841 census, the first to include personal names, there were some 70 people living in Tenby called Rees – and most of them were associated, directly or indirectly, with the sea. We need to cross reference the census returns with the St Mary's Parish Register and the names of his family as legatees in his will.

Lloyd et al 2004, National Archives St Mary's Register

Lexden Terrace about 1880. Tenby Museum and Art Gallery.

Our John Rees was baptised on 2nd December 1801 in St Mary's Tenby, the son of Thomas Rees, a sailor, and his wife, Ann Powell. Thomas was probably the Thomas Rees who captained *The Thomas* on the Tenby/Bristol run between 1800 and 1805, and *The Blessing* on the same route from 1805 to at least 1815. It may be through accompanying his father to Bristol that young John first encountered the seagoing ships in which he was to serve. We do not know much of Ann, but Thomas, lived to a good age. A letter to John Rees dated 1844 commiserates on his father's ill health and asks after him. We cannot find Thomas in the 1841 census of Tenby but there is a possible candidate (aged 75 in 1841) living in Wade Street, Bristol with the Harris family.

The will of John Rees, written in 1854, and the probate returns following his death in 1855 give us further clues to his life, in particular the sources of his wealth.

John Rees' estate was valued at £36,000, mainly in land in South Pembrokeshire including the Jeffreyston Estate, the Upper and Lower Loveston Estates, an estate in Llandissilio and 345 acres in Reynalton. The land was both agricultural and, in many cases, coal bearing. This valuation was for probate at acquisition cost, hence as low as his executors could justify, but still the equivalent of £3million today in purchasing power and ten times as much in relation to incomes and property values. In the middle of the century there was a statutory requirement for a magistrate to have an income from land of at least £100 a year and a legal definition of "Gentleman" as one of independent income; it was generally, however, reckoned that an income of £1000 a year was needed in order to properly support this designation. John Rees was a magistrate, a significant land owner and described himself as a gentleman; it is even more surprising, therefore, that so little is known about him and how he came by his property.

His wealth did not come from his family; the bequests of John Rees to family members which included annuities, suggest that they were not well off. Part of Rees' estate came from his wife; his estate includes £7,500 as a marriage settlement and £8,000 in trust for his wife from her (deceased) father These sums are intact on his death. He did not make his money like many in Tenby at the time, by exploiting the demand for holiday homes since he developed nothing except for his own use and sold little if any property in Pembrokeshire. There are three important clues in the will and in the associated estate papers: his bequest to Peter Butler; his naming of Harry Wright as executor and trustee, and the source of the money that he used for his land purchases, the London bank Magniac Jardine. John Rees had considerable funds with Magniac Jardine which were progressively transferred into property and stocks and shares over the five years from 1842. As late as 1846 there was nearly £11,000 still on deposit. Magniac Jardine was the bank set up by one of the principal China merchants, Hollingworth Magniac when he retired and returned to London. His independent Chinese trading company, or "Country Merchant" was bought out by William Jardine and James Mattheson and later renamed Jardine Mattheson, the name it still holds today. When William Jardine himself retired in 1839, he bought into Magniac's bank. As can be inferred from its origin, the main role of Magniac Jardine was to finance the China trade and to repatriate funds from China.

National Archives, Maitland Trust Papers, Thompson 1963, Rees Papers, LePichon 2006

Thus, we can conclude that John Rees was a Tenby man of relatively humble origins who became a self-made gentleman, having made his money in China. But when, and how?

Tenby Harbour, Henage Finch. Tenby Museum and Art Gallery

The Family

Thomas and Ann Rees had five children who survived to an age at which they could play a part in our story, Thomas, David, John, Mary and George (there is a family tree in Appendix III). Other children may have been born to Thomas and Ann; the St Mary's register is not helpful since there were several children born in Tenby at this time to parents called Thomas and Ann Rees, and it is difficult to unscramble the families. David Lewis Rees, baptised in 1800, became a master mariner, married a Bristol woman, Emily Wilcox and settled in Clifton with his family. His daughter, Elizabeth, married William Evans in 1857; his son David became a solicitor and did not marry. There are many mentions in the Rees papers to goods (such as half a barrel of sherry) being "put on your brother's boat". Although David was not one of the regular Tenby carriers such as William Rees of the *Star* (probably a cousin), there are indications that he was a ship owner and operator in the coastal trade and the reference must be to him.

National Archives, Rees Papers, Maitland Trust Papers, BMD

Mary, born in 1803, married a Tenby joiner, John Rowe, who died in 1840 leaving his wife to earn a living as a boarding house keeper. She had properties in Market Street and the High Street purchased with money that her brother, John, had lent. In 1841 she was living in Market Street with a young family: John 15, Sarah 11, George 9, Elizabeth 7 and Thomas 5. John Rees paid for the education of John Rees Rowe and George Henry Rowe and left the former his navigational books, charts and instruments and the latter his gold watch. They followed in their uncle's footsteps, becoming mariners in China; both died young – John Rees Rowe in 1857 in Hong Kong and George Henry Rowe in 1864 at Ning Po. Another daughter, in service in 1841, Mary Anne Rowe, married another John Rees in 1847. Their fate, and intelligence on what might have happened to Thomas David Rees, is suggested by an advertisement in the Melbourne Argus for 22nd March 1855: *Rowe T D of Tenby Pembrokeshire is requested to come or write to Williamstown immediately as his sister, Mary Anne and John Rees are about leaving for New Zealand.*

Maitland Trust Papers, National Archives, St David's, Welsh Mariners, BMD, National Library of Australia

Market Street Tenby in 1848 by Charles Norris, Tenby Museum and Art Gallery.
The buildings on the left were demolished shortly after to create a large open space, Tuder Square.

A Tale of Three Brothers

This story, however, is the story of the three remaining children, Thomas, christened in 1798, John in 1801 and George in 1805. Coming from what would appear to be an unremarkable background in a small town, all three were destined for a life of adventure at sea in China. Why did all three brothers follow this route? George may well have followed his brothers but Thomas, as the eldest, had no such incentive. There were many people in Tenby at the time with connections in India who might have given the necessary encouragement and introductions. William Paxton who did so much to develop Tenby, started as a country captain before moving into the more lucrative businesses of running the Calcutta Mint and of helping expatriates in India bring their money back to the United Kingdom.

However, the most likely connection is the Butler family. We have already mentioned Peter Butler. John Rees bequeathed: *"To my old and valued friend Peter Butler of Pembroke the sum of £50 as a token of regard"*. Peter Butler was the son of John and Lydia; they married in Bengal in 1796, she was not quite 14 years old and he was a country captain (a freelance merchant sailor) from a Castlemartin family. Peter, born in 1797, was followed by three more children before the Butlers returned to Britain – to Tenby – possibly because of the poor health of the youngest, Lydia Elizabeth, who died in 1804; her memorial tablet can still be seen in the aisle of St Mary's Church. At least two of the younger children, John (who became a Lieutenant-General in the Bengal Infantry) and George, were born in Tenby in 1804 and 1806. The next reference that we can find to the family in India is in 1812 when John senior died at sea, off Madras. Peter, a direct contemporary of Thomas Rees, became a country captain in India. In 1828 Peter Butler married Eliza Faddy, also born in Calcutta and by 1832 they had returned to Pembrokeshire, living on Main Street, Pembroke where, in 1847 and 1849, Peter Butler was Mayor. Did the Butlers establish a connection with the Rees family when they were in Tenby at the beginning of the century? Did John Butler give Thomas and John Rees introductions into the world of the country captain and their first openings, probably as captain's servant? In particular, did Thomas Rees and Peter Butler set off together to embark upon their career in the Far East? We have not as yet found firm evidence, but the obvious relationship which existed between John Rees and Peter Butler suggests that this was the case.

Rose 2000, India Office

Factories in Canton, about 1830.

The Factories were trading establishments with warehouses on the ground floor and offices and accommodation above.

Chapter 2   China Trade

There are many good and authoritative books upon trade with China in the early nineteenth century, in particular the opium trade, and the lead up to the Opium Wars. Several of these books are named in the list of sources.   What follows is merely an overview in order to provide a context for our story.

During the eighteenth and early nineteenth centuries, there was great demand for Chinese products in Britain, and also in Continental Europe and North America: silk, ceramics but mostly tea. At that time the tea plantations in India and elsewhere had not been established and China was the only source of tea in the form used as a beverage. But China was a difficult trading partner. It was ruled by the Manchu, Tartar invaders who had deposed the indigenous Ming dynasty in 1644. They ruled China through Tartar intimidation and corrupt mandarins. The Manchu were not popular and there were several attempts to reinstate the Ming. Like all despotisms, the rulers blamed dissent on outside influences: foreign products, technology and, most of all, ideas. They expelled the Jesuit missionaries, made it a capital offence to teach foreigners the Chinese language and closed the ports.

Beeching 1975

However, the opportunity of obtaining foreign currency, silver, in return for tea was too tempting. Trade was, therefore, permitted through Canton, governed by the Eight Regulations which had been drawn up with the objective of extracting as much money as possible from foreign merchants, whilst keeping them in such subjection that the danger of allowing them to come to China could be kept to a minimum. The most significant of these regulations was that all contact was to be with the Co-Hong and none with the Chinese officials. The Co-Hong was a group, generally eight or nine strong, of Chinese merchants who had bought the monopoly on foreign trade. They were based in Canton and the foreign merchants were allocated a piece of land next to the Pearl River, outside the walls of Canton, where they were permitted to establish their factories: "factories" being the name used for the warehouses, offices and accommodation needed to support trade. The remaining regulations represented petty restrictions upon the normal life and business of the foreigners which could be applied with greater or less force according to how uncomfortable their lives were to be made, and how restrictive the trade policy was to be.

British trade went hand-in-hand with the Industrial Revolution which supplied the manufactured items (mainly, at the time, textiles) that could be exchanged for trade goods – and just as manufacturing drove trade, so trade drove manufacturing by offering new and larger markets. But the formula broke down in the case of China which was self sufficient in textiles and only interested in trade in order to obtain silver. This created problems for The Honorable East India Company (HEIC), set up in 1600 with a monopoly on trade between Britain and the East Indies. Its monopoly, which had initially stretched from the Cape of Good Hope to the Straights of Magellan, had been eroded over the years and by 1813 was confined to China; even there, the only commodity for which the monopoly was enforced effectively, was tea. In the late eighteenth century the demand for tea had grown dramatically (in 1784, to reduce the incentive for smuggling, British Prime Minister William Pitt had reduced the duty on tea from 119% to 12.5%). At the beginning of the new century Britain had exhausted its foreign currency financing its Continental allies in the war against Napoleon. To add to the problems, available supplies of silver diminished as the Spanish West Indies, the principal source of monetary silver, sought independence from Spain. The HEIC was exhausting Britain's scarce silver reserves to satisfy the demand for tea.

Beeching 1975, Collis 1946, Napier 1995, Pettigrew 2003

The other traders active in the China trade at the time were other national trading bodies, such as that representing the Dutch, and the country merchants. And it was the country merchants who saved the situation in respect of the shortage of silver for the purchase of tea.

"Country" referred to local – the seamen and merchants who traded in the East Indies and were not involved with official bodies. With the erosion of the HEIC's monopoly, entrepreneurial westerners entered the market, joining the mainly Parsee country merchants to develop the trade within the "East Indies" and between East and West. However, all Europeans wishing to work in India, even if not in the service of the HEIC, needed to obtain its permission to reside in its settlements and to trade under the protection of its flag. Such men would go to India as country merchants, or, in the Rees case, as free-mariners aiming to become country captains. But one important difference between the captains employed by the HEIC and the country captains, was that the former were always accompanied by "supercargoes", traders employed by the HEIC, whereas the latter had to negotiate for themselves the best terms for the goods that they carried.   *Collis 1946 Le Pichon 2006*

It was the country merchants that saved the position with respect to the shortage of silver to purchase tea by developing a trade in commodities such as raw cotton from India.   The HEIC was saved by a triangular trade – tea from China to Britain, manufactures from Britain to India and commodities from India to China. But the country merchants were covetous of the HEIC monopoly on the tea trade with Britain and put pressure on the British Government to permit their participation.   Their success in finding an alternative to silver to fund the tea trade, and the HEIC's failure in this respect, gave the merchants the ammunition that they sought.

The country merchants, whilst seeking to have the remaining HEIC monopoly abolished, took comfort from its status as a quasi governmental body with a powerful navy of its own. Yet when the HEIC lost its monopoly in 1834 and ceased to trade, the country merchants and country captains became very exposed. In anticipation, in 1830 the British citizens in China, country merchants and captains, petitioned King William IV for British Government intervention and protection. The petition, which is reproduced as Appendix 1, gives a very clear view of the difficulties that they faced and of the steps that they thought appropriate. It is also the earliest document that we have found containing concrete evidence of John Rees' involvement in China.

Opium

The commodity side of the trade triangle described above was weak because it depended upon the vagaries of China's own harvests. But the country merchants were developing an alternative trade, that in opium. At this time opium was freely traded internationally; it was one of the few effective medicines available – a means of relieving pain and treating dysentery.   In the form of laudanum, opium resin dissolved in alcohol, it was very widely used and although there were problems with addiction, doctors did not feel able to relinquish so useful a drug. British imports of opium were 91000lb in 1830 (they were 280000lb in 1860). The eminent scholar and divine Isaac Milner, wrote to the anti-slavery campaigner, William Wilberforce who used opium against ulcerative colitis, *"be not afraid of the habit of such medicine, the habit of growling guts is infinitely worse"*.   The HEIC oversaw the auctions in Calcutta of the opium resin which was brought by the country merchants to China and sold for the silver which in due course paid for the tea shipped to Britain.

Collis 1946, Greenberg 1951, Hague 2008 Le Pichon 2006

The use of opium in China had started over a 1000 years earlier with that brought by the Arab traders, and developed with Turkish opium imported via the Portuguese settlement at Macao. But although expensive and hence initially confined to the mandarin class, the use of opium became a major social and economic problem. China banned trade in opium in 1729 and progressively tightened up the restrictions, but this was totally ineffectual since many of the government officials were both users themselves and keen to use the prohibition as a means of extorting money from traders, smugglers and addicts. During the late eighteenth century India became the most important source of opium. In 1773 the East India Company assumed a monopoly on the sale of opium originating in its dominions through the Calcutta auctions. Except for once, in 1782, when the Company was short of funds, it did not participate directly in the sale of opium to China. It did, however, arrange for the sale to the country merchants and benefited from their trade. The first British ambassador who had sought a trading agreement with the Chinese, Lord McCartney in 1793, had been empowered to offer suppression of the opium trade but, sadly as history unfolded, the Chinese government did not respond because they would not demean themselves by negotiating with barbarians. But as the nineteenth century advanced, the opium trade became more important to the British; the triangular trade (opium from India to China, tea from China to Britain and manufactures from Britain to China) became vital to the growing manufacturing industries and the profits on opium plus the tax on tea accounted for no less than one sixth of the combined revenues of Britain and India.

The trade was controversial in Britain but the general view was summed up by the first edition of the Catholic weekly, The Tablet, in 1840, which stated: *"Opium smoking is neither so prevalent nor so disgusting a vice in China, as gin drinking is in England. Now Lord Stanhope, if vested with power as large here, as the Emperor exercises in China, would certainly be quite as zealous in his desire to extinguish the filthy propensity of drunkenness among the lower classes of his own countrymen, as he appears to be solicitous to assist in the great moral reform of the Chinese. He would perhaps, for we rate his honesty more highly than his judgment, prohibit distillation at home, and impose some very severe penalties upon the importation of spirits from abroad."*

Collis 1946, Greenberg 1951, Grace 2006, Beeching 1975, LePichon 2006, Napier 1995.

It was under these circumstances that the trade in opium expanded. The merchants did not, other than in rare cases, smuggle the opium into China themselves, but took it to offshore locations (principally Lintin Island in the bay of Canton) where it was handed over to the Chinese smugglers who returned the silver that the merchants had previously exchanged for tea or silks.

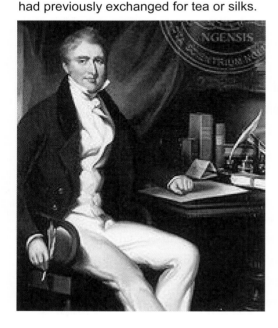

William Jardine 1784-1843

Jardine was known by the Chinese as the "iron-headed rat" and known to progress business by not permitting those who entered his office to be seated.

The leading opium merchant of the 1830s was Jardine Matheson formed in July 1832 out of an existing merchant company which had first originated in 1782 as Cox and Reid, becoming Magniac and Company in 1824. William Jardine was a ship's doctor who had served with the East India Company before joining Hollingworth Magniac, and James Matheson had previously assisted his uncle, a merchant in India. Jardine Matheson was, initially, a pure commission agent, taking 8% on the trades that it executed, but it soon started trading on its own account. The trades included textiles from Britain, rice and saltpetre as well as opium. When the EIC monopoly ended in 1834, Jardine Matheson was the first country merchant to bring tea to Britain.

The second most significant country merchant was Dent and Company which had arisen out of private venture trading by HEIC supercargoes. These had originally accompanied ships captains in order to execute trade but were expected from 1770 to remain in China. In 1831, Jardine Matheson and Dents accounted for two thirds of the private trade; there were three other firms and a dozen private individuals trading. John and George Rees worked for Jardine Matheson and Thomas Rees worked for Dent.

TheFalcon which became the flagship of the Jardine Matheson opium fleet in 1840.
It was captained by Francis Jauncey.

From Historia y Arqueologi Maritima

Chapter 3   The Brothers Rees in China.

This was the environment which the Rees brothers, Thomas, John and George joined. The 1830 petition addressed to King William IV in Council has already been mentioned. This petition (Appendix 1) requested the British Government to intercede with the Chinese authorities to eliminate what were seen as oppressive trading conditions for the British merchants. There were 47 signatories, comprising virtually the whole of the British community in China (which, in practical terms, meant Canton and Macao). One of those signatories was John Rees. However, this is not the earliest reference that we have to the Rees brothers in China and Thomas was to come to prominence before his younger brother.

Le Pichon 2006

Thomas

The first specific reference to the Rees brothers that we have been able to find in India or China is in 1826, when Thomas is shown as marrying a young widow, Maria Ann Woodhead in Calcutta Cathedral. He is described as a mariner and she, born Mary Ann Hedger in Calcutta in 1802, as the widow of Benjamin Woodhead – a Country Captain. Thomas and Maria had three children, Thomas Hedger (1828), Catherine Browne (1830) and Maria Hedger (1833). Lady Napier, wife of the British Government representative to China in 1834 was based in Macao; she wrote, *"there are the Captains of what are called the Country Ships, that is, traders between this and India, they are here during four months of every year and bring their wives, these are not all fine ladies, and being respectable, though not refined, I said that I should be happy to receive them and to return their visits"*.

STREET SCENE IN MACAO, c. 1829. From the original by George Chinnery R.H.A (1774-1852)

Mary Ann (by that time known as Maria) died in 1836 and is buried in the protestant cemetery in Macao.

British Library, Ride 1995, Napier 1995

By 1830 Thomas Rees was captain of the *Lord Amherst* a barque of 328 tons owned by Johnson & Meaburn and engaged in the China trade. In 1832 the Honourable East India Company chartered the *Lord Amherst* for one of the most significant expeditions it had ever mounted.

The Voyage of the *Lord Amherst*

Frustrated by the restriction on trade by the Chinese Government to the port of Canton, and realising that its lucrative tea monopoly was under threat largely because of its failure to trade British manufactures, the East India Company decided to test the trading situation along the Chinese coast. In particular, it wished to explore the possibilities of trade in Shanghai, the most important internal Chinese market. It established an exploratory mission comprising Hugh Hamilton Lindsay as leader and agent, Karl Gutzlaff as ship's doctor and translator, and Thomas Rees as Captain of the *Lord Amherst*.

Karl Gutzlaff 1803-1851

Gutzlaff was one of the most extraordinary characters of the period. Karl Friedrich August (Charles) Gützlaff, the Lutheran missionary, was born in 1803 in Pomerania, Prussia. He went to Batavia (now Jakarta) in the Dutch East Indies in 1826 and in 1831 embarked at Bangkok in a Chinese junk bound for Tianjin, China, subsequently making his home in Macao. In all of these travels he acquired a wide range of Eastern languages and was one of the few, if not the only, westerner to speak most of the variants of the Chinese language found along the coast. He dressed in the Chinese fashion and was even mistaken by the Chinese as one of their own. British traders began to make use of his extraordinary linguistic talents and he used the travels with merchants as a means of distributing Chinese language bibles and of making contact with the few, by then outlawed, Christian converts.

Collis 1946, Wylie 1867, Price

The East India Company did not wish to prejudice its position with the Chinese authorities and, hence, the operation was clandestine. This is why the Company chartered a typical country merchant ship instead of using one of its own, distinctive, East Indiamen. Lindsay was to pretend to be a country merchant blown off course, seeking shelter on the Chinese coast.

Gutzlaff's journal published in 1834 gives a full account of the expedition. Lindsay and Gutzlaff boarded the ship at Macao on 25th February 1832. The *Lord Amherst* carried a wide range of trade goods and sailed up the Chinese coast calling at any port which seemed to offer trading opportunities. The sailing was difficult and involved approaches along dangerous and (for Europeans) uncharted waters, especially at Shanghai where the shallows and islands in the mouth of the Yangtze made the approach without pilots very taxing. Lindsay and Gutzlaff spent 18 days on shore at Shanghai whilst Rees sailed to and fro, taking soundings and following the junks through the safe passages. Lindsay was to report: *"The charts of this part of the coast are very inaccurate; but I trust that the observations made by Captain Rees, as detailed by the chart exhibiting our track, will prove useful to future navigators in these seas"*. The adventurers continued north to Korea and returned via the islands of the China Seas, returning on 5th September. They had undertaken very little trade and the journey lost about £5000.

Gutzlaff and Lindsay reported that the people had received them well and that merchants were keen to trade with them but frightened to do so; the refusal of the Imperial Government to permit trade outside Canton was, for the most part, observed. They had obtained valuable intelligence and excellent charts – six of which are in the British Library today.

However, they also witnessed widespread opium addiction and were everywhere asked if they had opium to sell. There was demand for the one commodity that *The Lord Amherst* did not carry and it was Jardine Matheson that first and most vigorously responded to the opportunities revealed by the *Lord Amherst* expedition.

Gutzlaff 1834, Sutton 1981, Grace 2006, British Library

The Development of the Coastal Trade

Matheson had tried unsuccessfully trading up the Chinese coast on a previous occasion but with better intelligence and a tighter focus on opium, 1833 was to prove the start of what he later described as *"the golden years"*. Jardine Matheson took delivery of a fast clipper, *The Sylph,* just a few days before the return of *The Lord Amherst.* It arrived in Macao on its maiden voyage from India on 1 September 1832 in a record 18 days. On 20th October with a 70 man fully armed crew under Captain Wallace, *The Sylph* set sail from Macau into what Gutzlaff later described as *"furious gales and a tremendous sea".* This was followed by the *Colonel Young* under John Rees, the *John Biggar* captained by William McKay and, on 8th November the *Jamesina* with James Innes. William Jardine persuaded Gutzlaff to join as guide and interpreter; Gutzlaff was opposed to the opium trade but his co-operation was secured by financial support for his missionary work and the opportunity of using the company's vessels as a means of reaching the Chinese. He went out on the *Sylph* and returned on the *Jamesina.* One captain spoke of sailing up the Chinese coast, handing cases of opium over one side and bibles over the other.

From a picture of a country captain painted by George Chinnery in about 1830.
National Maritime Museum, London.

Grace 2006, Beeching 1975, Le Pichon 2006

The four ships that left Canton for the north mostly carried opium, although there were other trade goods and Gutzlaff in particular was charged with looking out for opportunities of trading in these – perhaps in deference to his scruples. Indeed, a letter from Gutzlaff to Jardine dated August 1833 makes the observation *"handkerchiefs are now in demand at a low price"*. However, handkerchiefs were a fig leaf for the truly profitable trade, in May 1833 William MacKay, now on board the *Sylph,* was reporting the sale of 267 chests of opium for $200,000, about £50,000 pounds.

The failure of the *Lord Amherst* expedition to sell trade goods signalled the end of the East India Company tea monopoly which happened, formally, in 1834. Jardine and Matheson realised that as a result competition in Canton would increase as new country merchants entered the market with a higher price for the purchase of tea and a lower one for the sale of opium. The real profits would be made by developing the coastal trade. They also realised that exploiting the coastal trade would demand a new system for the fast and efficient delivery of opium, since superior intelligence and more rapid response to the market would always put them ahead of the competition. Jardine Matheson had already started to invest in fast clipper ships which could sail in a hurricane and make two or three journeys a year between India and China as against the one for the lumbering East Indiamen. Ships such as the *Red Rover* delivered opium from Calcutta to Lintin where large receiving ships such as the *Hercules* stored it, and the *Sylph* and the *Fairy* carried the drug up the coast to larger, well armed ships such as the *John Biggar* and the *Austen.* These acted as floating trading posts, receiving on board the smugglers who bought the opium.

John Rees was appointed Commodore of the opium fleet which he ran from one of the larger ships up the coast.

George

And what of brother George? His career was not as well developed as that of his brothers. We first find him in 1838 sailing from Mauritius to Calcutta as master of the *Milford*. Between 1838 and 1840 he was in command of the *Austen*, a Jardine Mattheson ship, in 1838 being reported as discharging a cargo of opium at Lintin from India.

Le Pichon 2006, Ride 1995

Fort on the Canton River. 1832. George Chinnery. Based on an original in the British Museum

Chapter 4   Rees and his Gang.

John Rees, as the Commodore of the opium fleet and the man on the spot, had considerable discretion in opium trading.   A letter from William Jardine in 1838 reports of the purchase price of opium in various markets and goes on to say *"with this information before you we leave you to regulate prices according to your own views on the spot, and look forward to the result with perfect confidence".*   Gutzlaff also remained in the employ of Jardine Matheson and would often have been with John Rees to assist in negotiations with the local mandarins.   However, despite all of the courtesies, the real perception of John Rees is revealed in a PS to a letter from James Matheson to William Jardine dated 13/6/1839 during an interruption to the Canton trade: "***The coast trade promises fair – Rees and his gang are at work again".***

Le Pichon 2006, Greenberg 1951.

Opium was sold for cash and, as the Chinese outside Canton did not have the silver dollars handed over by the merchants in exchange for tea, the cash was a strange assortment of Spanish and Mexican Dollars, and many other currencies. John Rees collected coins and his experiences in China gave him many opportunities for building his collection – which he subsequently gave to his bride on their marriage. There was some barter and an 1835 letter from Jardine to Rees gives him advice on the quality of a sample of silk offered in return for opium. The most interesting diversion, however, was when John Rees helped George Gordon collect tea seeds.

Gordon was a member of the Tea Committee set up by Lord Bentinck, Governor General of India, to promote the cultivation of tea in India. This had the joint advantage of providing a valuable cash crop for India and reducing the dependence of the British on an uncertain trading partner. But only the Chinese had the varieties of tea that we liked to drink and only they knew how to process it. In 1834 Gordon sought the help of Jardine Matheson, firstly in obtaining the seeds and later in recruiting people to handle the crop. He was sent to join John Rees who was located nearer the tea growing areas and, no doubt, had valuable contacts with those who would help. Gordon collected 80,000 seeds which were planted in the Calcutta Botanic Garden and subsequently sent to Madras, Kuman and Assam where they provided the foundation of the Indian tea industry.

Shortly after Thomas Rees returned from his 1832 expedition up the coast of China in the *Lord Amherst*, the agents tried to sell the ship. They did not succeed and Thomas took a cargo to Australia before returning to Canton where the *Lord Amherst* was chartered by Dent. Initially used as a receiving ship in Lintin, the *Lord Amherst* was sent up the coast in the wake of the Jardine Matheson ships and in 1836 moored in Chimmo (or Shimmo) bay next to the *Colonel Young,* then captained by brother John. Jardine Matheson's profits demanded monopoly and Jardine himself encouraged John Rees to make things difficult for competitors who had followed him up the coast. He could do this by using his influence with the mandarins that he was bribing. Whether Thomas was a tougher competitor or whether John felt that he could not dismiss his brother, we do not know, but John and Thomas entered into a price fixing agreement and traded beside each other.

Le Pichon 2006, Greenberg 1951, National Archives, Ride 1995, JM Archive.

Thomas undermined his arrangement with his brother by giving the opium smugglers a discount to be paid on shore. When the double dealing was found out, Thomas became a persona non grata in the closed society of Canton and had to return to longer distance seafaring. By 1838 if not earlier he was back in command at sea, on the *Emily Jane* and then on the *Psyche* before retiring in 1842. Throughout, Thomas was supported by Dents on whose behalf he had broken the agreement, and they acted as executors and trustees on his death. Indeed, Dents as a company was not popular in the trading community and was often at odds with the other merchants.

Trading up the China coast was hazardous and John Rees and his associates survived because they were ruthless and used fast, well armed vessels. *The Sylph,* for example, was one of the first clippers, specifically designed for the opium trade. A barque rigged, square-sterned vessel of 300 tonnes, *The Sylph* had been designed in London by Sir Robert Sebbings, then surveyor of the Royal Navy, to the order of a consortium of Calcutta merchants. Sleek, elegant, functional and devoid of ornament, *The Sylph* did not have the rakish lines of the later clippers, yet it proved to be particularly swift. The country trade in opium between India and China had hitherto been conducted in the slow, corpulent, "country wallahs", constructed of Malabar teak in the shipyards of Bombay and on the Hooghly River near Calcutta. The country wallahs, like the equally cumbersome old East India frigates that carried tea, could only make one round trip to China per year. These ships could not sail into the monsoon, which dominates the China Sea between October and March. They generally took two or three months between India and Lintin Island, proceeding gently before the southwest summer monsoon, returning with the assistance of the stronger northeast monsoon of winter.

But even fast, well armed ships could not guarantee success when their cargos comprised valuable opium or silver. In 1836 the brig *Fairy* captained by a cousin of Jardine's, William McKay,and returning from the coast with substantial amounts of silver, disappeared. John Rees, then on the *Colonel Young ,* investigated and found that that the *Fairy* had been shipwrecked off a part of the coast notorious for pirates. Captain McKay and most of the crew had been killed. It was also suspected that the shipwreck was not accidental but caused by pirates who had infiltrated the crew.

JM Archive, Beeching 1975, National Archives, British Library, Warrane Lecture, Canton Register.

But although "Rees and his gang" were wary of piracy, they were also capable of acts of humanity. A letter in the Canton Register of 1835 reports on one such:

"Capt John Rees of the Colonel Young, whilst anchored in a bay near Chuan Chow, saw a junk run aground and break-up. He sent the longboat and rescued 14 men. He maintained them on the Young for a couple of days until the weather improved then sent them ashore with a few dollars to get home. Later some local villagers sailed out and presented Rees with joss sticks and red candles. A few of their number claimed money on behalf of those crewmen who had swum ashore themselves and not required rescuing but they were told to 'go away' ".

Three years earlier at Shanghai, Thomas Rees had saved a junk dismasted in a storm. This had helped to guarantee the toleration of the Chinese authorities when the *Lord Amherst* had spent over two weeks there.

Francis Jauncey

One of the key members of John Rees' gang was Francis Jauncey. In 1832 Jauncey had served under Thomas Rees on the *Lord Amherst* where he had helped in the preparation of the charts of the China coast. He later went to work for Jardine Matheson and, as the second most senior to John Rees, was offered the position of Commodore when Rees retired. An offer that he refused. Jauncey is also of interest in that he was a casualty of the only true battle in the run up to the opium wars; this occurred in 1840 when he was captaining a Jardine Matheson ship, the *Hellas.*
Matheson had agreed to help Captain Elliot, the British Government representative

in China, by *"penetrating the Yangtze Kiang to obtain channel marks for the Navel force."* The Chinese had placed underwater stakes to prevent the *Hellas* from turning. Eight junks sallied from the river to attack her with stink bombs and sought to board. They were driven off, but Hellas also withdrew to replenish her crew. Jauncey's jaw was smashed by a musket ball.

The schooner Hellas built at Dublin in 1832.

Beeching 1975, Le Pichon 2006, Rees Papers, Canton Register.

Jauncey was born in 1811 and christened in Dartmouth – his father, Captain Henry Jauncey was a captain in the Royal Navy, as was a younger brother, Horatio. One brother appears, however, to have followed Francis as we find him in an 1838 list of ships' officers in the Jardine Matheson archives – he was second officer of the *Lady Hayes* captained by Paterson, when Francis Jauncey was Captain of the *Governor Findlay*. John Rees kept in touch with Captain Jauncey and this gives us the only physical description that we have of Rees. In a jolly letter dated 12th July 1844 to John Rees in Tenby, Jauncey congratulated him upon his marriage and daughter, commiserated on the illness of his father and teased him about 'China Wallahs'. He also spoke affectionately of his correspondent as *"the little fellow"*.

The view of the Factories at Canton from the river. George Chinnery R.H.A. (1774-1852).

Harry Wright

In the will of John Rees the person named as his principal executor and trustee is, *"the Reverend Harry Wright of Cheltenham, formerly of China"*. Wright played a significant part in the Rees family's affairs, even (in his later capacity as a clergyman marrying John Rees' daughter to her fiancée, Frederick Maitland). Wright, born in London about 1812, the son of a London merchant, was a purser on the HEIC ship *Castle Huntley* before joining Jardine (then at Magniac) in 1826. He rose to become head of the opium department of Jardine Matheson and a partner in 1835.

Le Pichon 2006, JM Archive, IGI, Beeching 1975, Rees Papers, British Library.

Wright retired on 1st July 1842, travelling to Oxford where he studied as a preliminary to taking holy orders. He married Jane Haines in Bath in 1843; they had seven children. By the 1851 census he is described as a curate, living with his family and his father, Henry, at Hatherley Lawn in Cheltenham. Wright appears later as a clergyman without cure of souls living in Ilfracombe.

Robert Lungley

We have found throughout researching the history of John Rees that the associates of his China career continued to play an important part throughout his life. They even introduced him to the woman who was to become his wife, Emma Brown. The Ipswich Journal of June 15th 1839 announced the marriage on the 11th of Robert Lungley "*Late of Bombay*" to Amelia Brown. Amelia was Emma's younger sister and Lungley was almost certainly the R Lungley whose name appeared next to that of John Rees in an 1834 petition to the British Government.

The Lungleys were a family of China traders and mariners. A George Lungley was reported as a "free mariner" in Bombay in 1814 and either the same or his younger namesake sold the *Lady Hayes,* John Rees' old flagship, in 1854 before retiring to Boxford in Suffolk whence Robert had originated. In 1849, Dalrymple-Hay wrote:

"Between Macao and the Bogue is the Cumsingmoon anchorage. This was outside the boundary of the port of Hong Kong. It was a sort of No-Man's Land, in which neither Mandarin law, nor Portuguese law, nor Consular writ would run. In it were anchored the receiving ships both of British and American mercantile firms, and thither came to be supplied with opium and gunpowder, both lawful and unlawful traders. Among the ships at that time moored there, were the British ships. Lady Hayes, Captain George Lungley,........"

.

National Archives, BMD, JM Archive, British Library, Le Pichon 2006, Dalrymple Hay 1889.

The Nemesis destroying Chinese war junks during the Second Battle of Chuenpee, 7 January 1841

Edward Duncan (1803-1882)

Chapter 5   The Opium Wars

The country merchants continued to increase the coastal trade in opium – sales grew tenfold between 1802 and 1839 – but relations with the authorities in Canton became progressively more difficult. Whilst the The Honorable East India Company was the principal trade body, it could be regarded by the Chinese authorities as no more than another merchant – which met their refusal to deal with any governmental body – and by the other merchants as a governmental body which gave them a sense of security. But when the East India Company lost its monopoly of British/China trade at the beginning of 1834, there was a call for a British government representative to look after the interests of the British citizens. The first person appointed was Lord Napier who went to Canton despite being refused entry by the Chinese authorities who would not recognise an official appointment. He was blocked and obstructed at all stages (in the Chinese documents, the choice of ideograms used phonetically to represent his name translated as 'Laboriously Vile'). Napier became ill but the authorities in Canton which had tried so hard to exclude him would not allow an easy return to Macao. It was in Macao that he died on 11 October 1834.

Collis 1946, Greenberg 1951.

The Chinese became increasing concerned about both the social and economic implications of the growing opium imports and debated whether to legitimise the opium trade and make money from it, or to take more effective steps to enforce the ban. Lin Tse-hsu, who as Governor General of Hu-Kuang had succeeded in virtually eliminating opium addiction in his province, made proposals to the Emperor for the elimination of opium smuggling. On 31st December 1838 Lin was appointed Imperial Commissioner to Canton with full authority. His first act was to put the merchants under house arrest until they had handed over all the opium under their control, in the factories and offshore, and signed a bond undertaking never to deal in opium again. The bond provided that if they did, they would be executed and their crews would be strangled. Lord Napier's successor, Captain Elliot, representing the British government. stepped in to negotiate the handing over of 20,000 cases of opium, promising to indemnify the merchants, but insisting that no British subject would sign the bond since it would amount to consenting to be governed by Chinese law. An American trader, William Hunter, gave a first hand account: *"It is nothing more or less than an act of piracy. Not one of us is allowed to quit Canton, innocent or guilty, till the opium is all in his (Lin's) hands. He has caught us this time in a trap but please God he may be well thrashed for it yet, and if our lives, as he threatens, are to be the penalty for the non-delivery of the 20,282 chests of opium this place may by and by be made too warm for him".*

The situation became tense in Canton as security deteriorated and there were, initially, isolated acts of conflict. In 1839 Captain Elliot (who was, by that time, the British government representative overseeing British trade interests) ordered the British merchants to cease trading and to withdraw from Canton. There were rumours that Commissioner Lin and his troops would invade Macao with a view to seeking out the families of the British and putting them to death. The merchants sent their families to India and withdrew their businesses to the receiving ships moored in the Bay of Canton. The Chinese put prices upon the heads of the main players, including James Matheson, who announced his retirement from China. In fact he continued running the business but under a false name, from the *Hercules,* off Hong Kong, then a quiet fishing village.

Collis 1946, Beeching 1975, Hunter, Waley 1958.

It is a tale which, in all of its complexity is well told in a number of publications, some of which are detailed in the bibliography. Our purpose, however, is simply to trace this part of the story insofar as it affected the Rees brothers and was contributed to by them.

In September 1839, John Rees submitted his resignation from Jardine Matheson. James Matheson replied from the *Hercules* on 28th September 1839, accepting. The letter was unsigned; a note in another hand saying that this was *"in case the letter fell into the hands of the Chinese"*. The letter is worth quoting in full since it throws light upon John Rees standing and the organisation of the company.

> *My dear Sir,*
>
> *in acknowledging that part of your letter of 13th September announcing your wish to retire, I cannot but express our regret at losing the services of so useful and zealous a Commander as you have always proved. It would be most unreasonable however were we to put any obstacle in the way and you have accordingly our full assent to carrying into effect the requisite arrangements for the purpose whenever it may best suit your convenience. Captain Jauncey as next to you in seniority and having always enjoyed our entire confidence and good opinion will naturally have the option of succeeding you in the 'Lady Hayes' but as the state of the Singapore market will render it necessary for him to proceed to Calcutta, he cannot be expected back till February and it will therefore be necessary to make a provisional arrangement to prevent you being detained till then. Captain Hall being the next in seniority to Jauncey we propose his succeeding him in the 'Hellas' and that Mr Forbes shall take command of the 'Harriet' till Jauncey return we leave it to you to make such provisional arrangements as you deem proper. Due subordination will be best preserved by Captain Hall at once taking the provisional command of the 'Hayes' till Jauncey returns and giving Mr Forbes the 'Harriet'. But should you see inconvenience in this course from difficulty with the crew, or otherwise, we leave you to make such other arrangements as you deem fit. Mr Holmes proceeds in the 'Henrietta' to take the vacant Chief Officers berth.*

Rees Papers - D/EE/55/60

Although James Matheson had pretended to retire in order to escape the Chinese, William Jardine had really retired earlier in 1839 and was on a leisurely trip back to the UK when trouble developed. But he was prepared and had with him copies of the charts and documentation which had been assembled on the Chinese coast, both from a navigational and military point of view. Indeed, there are some indicators that Jardine and Matheson had long wanted to precipitate a war with China in order to compel an open trading regime – they now had an excuse. But Jardine had to proceed with caution; there was little sympathy in Britain for opium traders and no stomach for war just to enable them recover the cost of the opium that they had been compelled to surrender to the Chinese. Benjamin Disraeli summed up the general feeling in his contemporary novel, Sybil: *"Oh! A dreadful man! a Scotsman, richer than Croesus, one McDruggy, fresh from Canton, with a million of opium in each pocket, denouncing corruption and bellowing free trade."*

Jardine played upon the ambitions of the leaders of the textile industries of Manchester and Glasgow that somewhat optimistically looked to China as their next big market and brought them to support him in demanding action against the Chinese. He played upon national pride, outraged by the thought of British citizens being oppressed by a foreign power.

Lord Palmerston (1784-1865). First became a Minister in 1809 and served in both Tory and Whig administrations, latterly as Prime Minister, until shortly before his death.

William Jardine sought an interview with Lord Palmerston, then Foreign Secretary, and advocated military action, handing over all of the intelligence that Jardine Matheson had gathered on the state of coastal defences in China *"that his Lordship might have a clear idea of the country with which we must cope"*. Lord Palmerston kept the charts drawn by Thomas and John Rees, to show the Cabinet when it met on the Monday following.

JM Archive, Le Pichon 2006, Greville 1875

The Government was initially reluctant to embark upon an adventure so far from home but Jardine had been skillful in generating support for action against the Chinese and had also persuaded Palmerston of its practicality. The decision was taken to send an expeditionary force, proceeding from India, to reach Canton about March 1840. The Whig Government of Lord Grey was aware that despite Jardine's efforts there would be opposition in Parliament and the Country so, instead of taking the proposal to Parliament, the Government decided to use the resources of the East India Company; this did not require parliamentary approval. When Palmerston eventually sought Commons authority for the first expedition to China, Sir James Graham, moving the vote, estimated that one sixth of the combined revenue of Great Britain and India depended upon the China Trade. British import duties amounted to £4.2 million and India earned £2m. The debate was heated but there was little opposition to the expedition – things had gone too far. However, there was strong opposition to a government which had permitted this state of affairs to arise and a parallel motion of censure was proposed and defeated by only nine votes

Battle at Guangzhou, Second Opium War.

Grace 2006, Collis 1946, Beeching 1975.

The initial commander of the British troops, as the man on the spot, was Captain Charles Elliot but he was felt by all of the British community (with the interesting exception of James Matheson) to be too conciliatory. Elliot was replaced in 1841 by the former Indian Army General Sir Henry Pottinger who was anything but conciliatory; he compelled the Chinese to sign the Treaty of Nanking in 1842 which created five free ports, ceded Hong Kong to Britain and provided for substantial reparations for the British Crown and the British merchants. In the correspondence between Jardine and Matheson it is recorded that one of the people who briefed Pottinger before he travelled to China was Captain John Rees.

Le Pichon 2006, Pottinger 1997

South Gate (Five Arches) Tenby, Charles Norris. Tenby Museum and Art Gallery.

Chapter 6   Return Home

Although John Rees resigned in September 1839 and, as the letter quoted above shows, James Matheson did not seek to detain him, we do not know exactly when he returned to the UK. In *The Times* for 4th July 1840 a report from Macao dated 20th March mentions that Rees is "*on the east coast with the Lyra, Harrier and Water Witch*". A letter from William Jardine to James Matheson dated 3rd March 1841 reported the publication of Lord Jocelyn's "*Six Months with the Chinese Expedition*" saying that Jocelyn had expressed his opinions to John Rees on board the steamer returning from India – presumably at the beginning of 1841. In the 1841 Census (April), Rees is living in Commercial Square, Stepney (next to the East India Dock) in lodgings, probably having landed not long before.

Le Pichon 2006, Rees Papers, National Archives

John Rees next took a rather grand house in Bristol, 12 Caledonia Place, Clifton, where the newly opened Great Western Railway provided fast access to London and the sea provided somewhat slower access to Tenby. But he clearly intended to return to Pembrokeshire and started to buy land – on July 14th 1842, John Gwynne, Solicitor, had John Rees added to the voters list of Llandissilio on the basis of his property qualifications.

The correspondence studied would suggest that, quite rightly, John Rees was seen as somewhat of an expert on China and that his opinion was sought by many. Yet, as already noted, none of this reputation was carried over into Pembrokeshire – local sources appear to make no mention of his background. Why was this? With the change from the Georgians to the Victorians, attitudes in Britain were also changing. The Georgians and the Whigs were libertarian but the Anglican Church, the Tories and, ultimately, the Victorians in general thought that it was morally wrong to support opium traders and to go to war, largely to enforce reparations for the loss of opium stocks. By the time that John Rees returned to Tenby, respectable people would not have wished to associate with an opium trader. Which may be why the story of John Rees' time trading opium for Jardine Matheson has been lost until now.

Thomas

Thomas Rees retired in 1842 and returned to the UK as a passenger in the *Sir Herbert Compton*, settling in Brighton rather than Tenby. Why Brighton? One possibility is that, after the incident of Chimmo Bay he did not wish to meet his brother in Tenby. The second is that he was meeting, by arrangement, Louisa Marquis, the daughter of Thomas Marquis, a retired HEIC Commander, since, in January 1843, they were married in Brighton. Thomas died in summer of that year leaving Louisa expecting Mary Ann. He may already have been unwell when he returned since in his will there is a bequest to an attendant, Fishburn Shaw, a one time boatswain with the HEIC Maritime Service.

Le Pichn 2006, Rees Papers, Grace 2006, National Archives Fibis.

Thomas Rees' wealth was left in trust for the benefit first of Louisa, provided that she brought up all of his children, and then for the children themselves. Louisa Rees travelled to India, taking Mary Ann with her, returning to London in her old age. Thomas Hedger Rees, the only son, became a lieutenant in the Honorable East India Company in 1846 and in 1853 is recorded as serving with the 16th Regiment of Native Artillery in Bombay. Young Thomas was a residual beneficiary under John Rees' will and married in Bombay in 1864; we do not believe that he ever returned to Britain to settle. Catherine married a clergyman, Joseph Hodgett, in Clifton in 1860. Young Maria also returned to the UK and married a clergyman in Clifton (1861), John Cox Edwards. Mary Ann, daughter of Louisa stayed in India and married Frederick Greenway in 1862.

George

Thomas Rees may not have returned to Tenby, but his brother, George, never even returned to the UK. By December 1841 he was in command of the brig *Royal Exchange* at Canton which was chartered to and operated by Jardine Mattheson. George had purchased a 16/64 share in the *Royal Exchange*; this was quite common and companies such as Jardines extended mortgages for this purpose – although both the rates and the risks were high. According to *The Cambrian* newspaper of 4th February 1843. in a notice probably placed by John Rees, George Rees died *"very suddenly, from a stroke of the sun, on 27th September last, on board of the brig Royal Exchange, at Hong Kong"* . He left everything to John, including his share of the *Royal Exchange*. Why would George leave everything to his wealthiest relative? As John Rees himself was in funds, it would have been natural for him to have lent his brother the money to buy into a ship and on his brother's death, the asset would have reverted to John. A friendly agreement reflected in the will (George had no dependents) would have been less complicated than a formal mortgage. John Rees was also better placed than anyone else in the family to recover George's assets from China.

National Archives, British Library, Ride 1994, Swansea Library.

George Rees' will was in a verbal form, attested by witnesses and proved by affidavit since on 23 January 1843, the Tenby solicitor John Gwynne working for John Rees tried, unsuccessfully, to help Mary Rowe find *"your Brother's will but I could not find it in your iron chest or the box".* Jardine Mattheson handled George's affairs, corresponding through Magniac Jardine. David Lewis Rees and John Rees signed a letter of attorney to Jardine Mattheson permitting the sale of the *Royal Exchange* by the East India Company. There were matters outstanding as late as 28th October 1844 when Jardine Mattheson wrote to John Rees following an enquiry from him saying: a book *"kept on the Royal Exchange and sent under the care of Captain Woodworth of the barque Marchioness of Douro to clear up matters of doubt. With regard to the chop put on board the Lady Hayes* (the ship commanded by John Rees at his retirement in 1839) *we presume it was under the care of Captain Patterson of the ship between whom and your late brother there was a private understanding of which you are already aware".* Although the above is not clear, it does illustrate the complexity of the affairs of the Country Captains and the opportunities that they had for private enterprise; the word 'chop' was used for a package of a commodity, usually tea.

Grave of George Rees photographed in the Protestant Cemetry, Macao.
By kind permission of Ena Neidergang.

Rees Papers

Marriage

During his time in London John Rees would have met with his old colleague, Robert Lungley, in his house in Fitzroy Square. At the time of the 1841 census, his wife's older sister, Emma, was living with them. Emma Brown was born on 28th February 1802 and christened at the Lion Walk Meeting House at Colchester. Her father was Bartholomew Brown of Church House Farm, in the village of Lexden, just outside Colchester; described as a farmer in Emma's marriage certificate and a merchant in his will, (a corn and coal merchant according to Piggott's Directory of 1823). Bartholomew Brown died in 1838 leaving his family well provided for. The family tree is in Appendix III; we know a little about Amelia Lungley and three sons, Bartholomew the farmer and landed proprietor who went to live in Ramsgate, Stephen, a silk frowster and Colchester magistrate, and Samuel Simons, a corn merchant who ended at Belsize Park, London. Their mother, Sarah lived until nearly 90 in St Mary's Terrace, Lexden Road, Colchester.

We have not been able to find out what Emma Brown did in her adult life before 1842 but she may have been active in the public good; she was a strong non-conformist, and a strong Liberal according to an interview given by her daughter to the *Women's Penny Paper*. Emma Brown was clearly a capable businesswoman with control of her own affairs. Her father had left her a one fifth share in the disposal of a parcel of property including houses, a malting yard and the Nelson public house in Colchester. She invested widely, including in Brighton Railway Bonds and shares in The Colchester Gas Light and Coke Company. It is also revealing that Emma's draft will of 1838 included a bequest of £1,000 to Amelia for *"her sole use and free from use or debts of her present or future husband"*.

During her time at Tenby, Emma's main contacts appear to have been with the family and friends from her Colchester time. According to the Tenby Visitor's List the Misses Brown and the Misses Lungley often stayed with their aunt.

Maitland Trust, National Archives, IGI, Rees Papers, Tenby Observer, Woman's Penny Paper.

The Welshman newspaper reported on The Master of Ceremonies' Ball in the Tenby Assembly Room, probably on August 25th 1842, giving a list of those present which included Captain Rees and Mrs and Miss Brown. On 11th October 1842 John Rees married Emma Brown at St George's, Hanover Square, London; both were aged 40 and both previously unmarried. There was a marriage settlement of £7,500 – John Rees settled £4,500 in 3% bank annuities on Emma plus £3,000 in new 3½% annuities and a reversionary share of certain trust monies – under the law at the time this recognised that Emma's own property (which was probably of similar value) came to John Rees. John also gave Emma his coin collection, examples of the disparate money that he would have acquired from the coastal Chinese anxious to buy opium.

The Croft, Tenby c 1864. Tenby Museum and Art Gallery.

John and Emma Rees settled at 7, The Croft, Tenby and it was there that their first child, Emma Knox Rees, was born on 17th May 1844.

Price 2006 Maitland Trust, National Archives, Rees Papers.

Early nineteenth century postcard of

Caldy Island showing the castle ruins on the left and Green Gardens House on the right

Chapter 7   Tenby Life

On 5th November 1842 John Rees purchased Green Gardens from the trustees of Elizabeth Bateman, deceased, for a price of £1230. The estate had been divided into five lots and auctioned at the White Lion Inn on 6th June 1842. Green Gardens comprised Green Garden House and a row of cottages including a shop. On September 29th 1842, John Gwynne, solicitor, served notice on the tenants of Green Gardens which included George Mends – a joiner who later became a prominent citizen and Councillor. Green Gardens House was one of the premier residences in Tenby and we do not know whether Rees initially intended to live there or whether he always intended to develop what became Lexden Terrace.

Walker, Rees Papers.

John Rees continued to invest heavily in land in the County. In addition to Green Gardens, he purchased Haywood Meadow from the trustees of Elizabeth Bateman and, in the following year, land in Frog Street from Charles Cook Wells where he built three cottages – Lexden Cottages. In 1847 he purchased the Jeffreston Estate, the Upper and Lower Loveston Estates, the Rydenoch Estate in Llandissilio, 345 acres including woods and plantations in Reynoldson and various other parcels of land. The total cost of this land was £15,780. John Rees also made a number of leasehold investments – including Jeffreston House which was subdivided in 1851 and occupied by a publican and two families of coal cutters. By 1852 the Frog Street premises were too small for the associated offices of the Rees family and he leased land from the Council in St John's Croft for stables and offices (14 years at £35 a year). At his death he had two carriages stabled there.

Jeffreston House

Apart from the Tenby properties, his investments were all on the Pembrokeshire coal field. Did John Rees invest for the coal deposits or for the agricultural income? The limited evidence suggests that he obtained revenues from both; they were probably opportunistic investments. On the other hand, we have found no evidence of John Rees selling any property. The picture that comes across is of a self-made man who sought to establish himself as a gentleman through the ownership of land – in the mid nineteenth century no matter how wealthy you were, you were not looked upon as being a gentleman unless the bulk of your income came from land. There was even a legal definition of "Gentleman" as "one who had no occupation" and John Rees described himself as a Gentleman after his return from the Far East.

Maitland Papers, National Archives, Thompson 1963

As a major landowner, Rees inevitably became a magistrate and shortly after he returned to Tenby he was asked to chair a committee set up to put pressure on the operators of steam packets between Tenby and Bristol to reduce their fares in order to encourage traffic. The Committee announced that it would set up a fund for the establishment of a Tenby owned packet company whereupon The Bristol Steam Navigation Company caved in and reduced its cabin fares from 25/- to 17/6. The Pembrokeshire Herald of 19th July 1844 reported an event arising from this exercise which gives a good flavour of Tenby at the time. *"On Thursday 12th inst., John Rees Esq, chairman of the committee for reducing the fares of the steam-packets plying between Tenby and Bristol, was invited by the committee to a dinner at the White Lion Hotel. About forty gentlemen, comprising the members of the committee and other friends of Mr Rees were present on the occasion. The chair was ably filled by Wilbraham Falconer Esq., M.D.; the vice chair by Mr William Harries. After the usual loyal and patriotic toasts, the chairman proposed the health of John Rees, Esq. and in doing so dwelt upon the energy, impartiality and decision which that gentleman had shown in the discharge of his duties as chairman of the committee; also on the public advantages derivable from his residence in this place; and incidentally referring to the new buildings, Lexden Terrace, lately erected by Mr Rees on the South Cliff. The toast was received with reiterated cheers. Mr John Rees acknowledged the compliment in a brief but appropriate and expressive manner. Several toasts of a convivial nature followed and the evening was enlivened by the strains of vocal harmony volunteered by Messrs William Harries, Rolland, Henton, J. Owen, J. Smith, Capt Rees of the Star steamer, and others."*

Other than this and as a resident, we found John Rees' name in either the Tenby Observer or the Pembrokeshire Herald on only one occasion; in 1854 he was the biggest contributor (10 gns) to the fund to pay for the new cemetery and chapel of rest. John Rees was also an active member of the Independent Chapel, The Tabernacle, in Frog Street

Pembrokeshire Herald, Tenby Observer, Rees papers

However, John Rees was not beyond being 'landed' with something; Wilbraham Falconer of Stoat Hall, Swansea, made him the President of the Tenby Literary and Scientific Society. Falconer wrote Rees the kind of letter that you cannot say "no" to, when writing to say that he was compelled to resign the position and trusted that Rees would take it up in his stead. The Literary and Scientific Society appeared to be a cross between reading rooms and a self-improvement group; it rented rooms and subscribed to such periodicals as *The Builder, The Mechanics Magazine, The Times, Daily News, Punch* and *Chambers Journal.*

Fatherhood

On 17 May 1844 Emma Rees gave birth to their first and only child, Emma Knox Rees. The name "Knox" may have come from George Knox who was a trustee under Bartholomew Brown's will and a witness at the Rees wedding. Young Emma later described her childhood thus. *"As a child I was very fond of studying. I was educated by governesses at home until I was 12 and then went to a boarding school."* The school was in Powis Square, Brighton and run by the three Misses Elwall. With two other resident teachers and visiting masters teaching science and mathematics, the 12 resident girls benefited from an extraordinary staff pupil ratio. She also said *"I was also much interested in politics from childhood.........my mother was a strong liberal and I inherited her earnest convictions".*

In 1854 John Rees wrote his will. Apart from some personal bequests to his family and to Peter Butler, the bulk was left for the benefit of his wife and then of his daughter and of her family. But the will was written before the Married Woman's Property Act and is complex in setting up a trust whereby his wife would lose the benefit of all but a few personal bequests if she remarried. The "beneficiaries" (trustees) are Harry Wright ("Harry Wright of China") and William Matthias Jones, Surgeon of Tenby. Jones dropped out and Emma Rees was named in this capacity provided that she did not remarry.

National Archives, Pembrokeshire Herald, DNB, Womans Penny Paper

John Rees died on 24th February 1855. He asked to be buried without fuss, wherever he happened to die, but if he died in Tenby he was to be buried in the vault that he had purchased for his wife, daughter and himself. He is buried in the Tenby cemetery in a vault intended for three – but containing only John Rees himself.

Emma Rees took over the over the running of the estate, living alone in 1 Lexden Terrace with occasional visits from her Brown and Lungley relatives. In 1861, when Emma Knox reached 17 she decided to take her to St Tropez for the winter, with her cousin, one of Robert and Amelia's daughters, probably Catherine Lungley who was then 19. Emma Rees was taken ill after an exhausting diligence drive from Toulon, it was likely to have been cholera which was then rife on the Riviera, although not spoken of lest it harmed the tourist trade. She did not speak French and was nursed by the girls for twelve days before dieing on 7 November 1861.

Frederick Maitland was a family friend who had stayed with the Rees family in Tenby the previous summer. It had been agreed that he should join the party in St Tropez and his arrival shortly before Emma's death was clearly a great help. Maitland was said by Emma Knox to be looked upon by her mother as a son; on her deathbed (according to a letter written by her daughter) she joined their hands together and commended Emma to Frederick's care. Emma and Frederick announced their engagement on the day following Emma senior's death.

Memorial to Emma Rees in the Cemetery at St Tropez   *Courtesy Leonard Rees*

Maitland Papers, National Archives.

Harry Wright left Cheltenham for St Tropez as soon as he heard of the death, but by the time he arrived, everything had been organized by Frederick Maitland. Emma Rees was interred in the cemetery in St Tropez, overlooking the Mediterranean Sea.

Robert Lungley took exception to the match and wrote to Harry Wright to see if they had grounds to overturn it, or to buy Maitland off. Lungley seemed especially irritated in that Emma's will provided for £9,500 (which was substantially the whole of her personal estate outside her husband's trust) to be paid to her daughter's husband if she, the daughter, married before the age of 21. He would have been the guardian of Emma Knox had she not married and seemed to consider that the unusual provision of Emma senior's will would have the effect of depriving his daughters of benefits to which he thought them entitled. But Emma Knox Rees was determined, as testified by the tone of the letter announcing her engagement and written to the family solicitor within 24 hours of her mother's death. However, the death of Emma senior did lead to the need for an additional trustee under John Rees' will and Harry Wright appointed Robert Lungley.

Emma Knox Rees and Frederick Maitland were married on 21st July 1862 in Cheltenham by the Reverend Harry Wright. One of the guests at the wedding was a young solicitor from Haverfordwest, Edward Eaton Evans, and he continued looking after Emma's affairs until he was 80; the papers deposited by his company with the Pembrokeshire County Public Record Office are amongst the principal source documents of this account.

Maitland Trust, National Archives,.

Lexden Terrace pre 1868, Tenby Museum and Art Gallery.

Chapter 8   Lexden Terrace

On 5th November 1842 John Rees purchased *Green Gardens*, and the Council Minutes Book for 11th April 1843 quote him as stating *"it is my intention to erect a terrace of 5 or 6 houses on my property called Green Gardens in St Julian Street opposite The Hope and Anchor"*.   Permission was granted and the Corporation agreed to *"stop up the nuisance near your property on condition of your giving them six feet of road"* for widening St Julian Street.   Rees' solicitor John Gwynne had already prepared a contract for the building of five houses and advised upon an invitation to tender being put in *The Carmarthen Journal,* but it would appear that John Rees entered into immediate negotiations with John Smith.

Tenby Museum, Rees Papers.

The contract commenced on 15th April and provided for John Smith to continue in employment if the houses were covered in by 15th November; John Rees could not have pushed ahead at this rate if he had had to go through a tendering process. The contract, provides that "*John Smith mason agrees with Mr John Rees to provide good and sufficient labour to pull down*" Green Gardens and to dispose of the materials. He was to be reimbursed upon a day rate, "*no beer allowed*". The contract provided for the building of five new houses to be built according to plans to be let out by contract to the lowest tender, subject to John Rees approving each contractor. Masons, bricklayers and plasterers were to be sourced and paid by Smith, carpenters and joiners by Rees. All materials were to be found by Rees. If the houses were covered by November 15th, John Smith was to be kept on at 18s a week, if not, at Rees' discretion. Each was to keep a day book and John Rees supervised the building on a daily basis. Rees paid Smith a total of £3,174 for the construction of five houses. By March 1844 the first two houses, 5 and 4, were ready to be painted and varnished.

The name, Lexden Terrrace, is, of course, in recognition of Emma Rees' place of birth and they are feminine houses in feel, it could be that Emma had a hand in selecting the design. And they are designed rather than put up by a builder to a specification since we know that drawings existed prior to Smith being involved and there is a grace and confidence visible in the interior in particular that suggests architectural competence. The design was not created for the Tenby site; the style was at least 20 years out of date when the houses were built, there are details that suggest that the original dimensions were compressed in order to fit 5 houses onto the site and there were several small changes to adjust Regency show to Victorian comfort. The only architect with whom we know that John Rees had dealings (and that was 1846) was Samuel Burleigh Gabriel of Clifton, near Bristol. Gabriel had Indian connections, lived close by John Rees in Clifton in 1842 and Gabriel's sister Dorothy married Charles Gutzlaff, one of Rees' closest associates in China, when the latter made a fleeting visit to the UK in 1850. It seems possible that Gabriel produced drawings for Rees based on an earlier design or even existing house.   *Rees Papers, BMD, National Archives.*

The model is to be found in spa and seaside towns from nearly a generation earlier. By 1844 when the houses were nearly completed, a correspondent to *The Welshman* described John Nash, the architect who was the epitome of this style, as *"an execrable architect, devoid of taste, genius, originality, infatuated with self-conceit and fit only to pander to the depraved longings of a tasteless age."* The houses follow the Nash model of a vaulted entrance hall that looks straight through via door and window to a vista beyond, with a fine staircase hall offset from this axis containing an elegantly curved staircase illuminated by a circular rooflight. But Victorian standards of comfort and privacy placed internal double doors across the vista.

Externally, at the back a once open terrace (since partitioned and shared between the now individually owned houses) overlooks a common garden known as "the pleasure ground", and beyond that the sea. At the front, where cars now park, there was a circular carriage drive entered from gates on St Julian Street.

The entrance to Lexden Terrace from St Julian Street. No 1, where John Rees lived, is the first house on the right.

John Rees lived in No.1, adjoining the entrance gates, the largest house of the five. This would be consistent with a terrace built primarily as a means of generating income. But the Rees family was wealthy and did not need to acquire close neighbours purely for financial reasons. Did they, therefore, decide to control their environment for social reasons, to live with people with whom they felt comfortable? It appears that Rees would have known some of the early tenants and also that he was, initially, very opposed to subletting.   *Suggett 1995, Rees Papers.*

This was illustrated by an incident described in his solicitor's accounts (which, incidentally, also gives an insight into the character of John Rees). On 4th March 1845 Robert Harris took a short lease on No.3 for £52.10s a year. However by June 1846, Harris was subletting and Rees was incensed, spending a great deal of time with the solicitor, John Gwynne, looking through the lease to see if he could take action against Harris and his tenant, eventually resorting to serving a notice saying that *"the lodger that he agreed to take in not to have the pleasure of walking on the pleasure ground and that should any damage be done to the water closets and pipes"* Harris would be answerable. On June 30th Harris said that he would disregard the notice and might cancel his lease. On August 14th John Gwynne was sent by Rees to speak to the tenant, Colonel Bagnold, reading out the paragraph in Harris' lease which expressly forbade friends to walk in the garden – pointing out that this meant that Bagnold and his family were not permitted in the pleasure ground. The Colonel *"seemed very much surprised"* and said that he would refer to his landlord. The eventual outcome is not recorded but Harris certainly did not retain the property for the standard lease term of 7 years.

A comparison of the leases with the census shows that there were often residents other than those to whom the houses had been let. Information on occupants is available from census returns although these only give information at ten year intervals and on those in residence at the time of the census, thus excluding family away from home and staff living out. Electoral registers identify male residents, and tenancy agreements and correspondence are an invaluable but patchy source. The Tenby Observer gives information on those visitors who left their cards with Richard Mason, its proprietor, and this suggests that between 1853 and 1860 there was a constant procession of visitors to No.2 during the holiday season, but not to the other houses. It might be concluded from all of this information that whatever Rees' original intention, he had to become reconciled to the houses being largely used as holiday homes and often sublet, and may even have profited from this demand himself.

Maitland Trust, Rees Papers, National Archives, Electoral Registers.

There were some permanent residents. James Pickering Ord of Bath was one and on 3rd April 1846 John Rees leased No.5 to him for a period of seven years at a rent of £45 a year. Ord, a man of independent means born in County Durham, died at the age of 72 in 1863, still living at No.5. From his census returns it is possible to see the level of staffing that would have been expected in houses of this kind. In addition to Ord, his wife, Isabella, and his daughter Ann, there were four servants living in the house, a butler, housekeeper, cook and housemaid. There were probably others not resident and the census returns for the Hope & Anchor public house opposite shows many lodgers described as servants.

The other residents, whether permanent or temporary, were of the same kind, wealthy individuals and minor gentry, some from Pembrokeshire but others from all parts of the United Kingdom. Early residents also included a surprising number of widows, perhaps responding to the feminine aspect of the houses.

Maitland Trust, Rees Papers, National Archives.

Lexden House on the north east side of Lexden Terrace is frequently thought to have been part of the original development and to have been the home of John Rees. It was, in fact a slightly later development by a Tenby woman, Rachel Williams, whose family house adjoined Green Gardens. She originally termed it No.6 Lexden Terrace and the designation "Lexden House" was assumed after its purchase in 1867 by Charles Henry Smith, a mine owner from Swansea.

Hutton

Lexden Terrace showing Lexden House.

The Rosslyn Hill Unitarian Chapel, Hampstead, where most of John Rees' grandchildren were christened.

Chapter 9 Descendants

Emma Knox Rees, the only child of John and Emma Rees, married Frederick Maitland on 21st July 1862 in Cheltenham. They did not stay in Tenby but sold up and moved to Croydon, where one of Maitland's older brothers lived. At the sale held at No 1 Lexden Terrace on 29th and 30th January 1862, the principal purchaser was the new tenant, Frederick Craven. However, virtually the whole of Tenby appear to have turned out and to have bought something, if only an inkwell for one shilling.

Frederick Maitland was older than his new wife (Emma was born in 1844), having been christened on 20th April 1823 at the Independent Chapel in Walworth Locks Field. His father, Joseph (and possibly earlier generations of his family) worked for the Honourable East India Company becoming Chief Clerk in the Examiner's Office in London (where correspondence was dealt with), before retiring in 1854. Sir Richard Burton, the celebrated explorer, obtained a cadetship in the East India Company on the recommendation of Joseph Maitland. The family tree is in Appendix III.

Maitland Trust, BMD, National Archives, Bible, Godsall 2008, Howard 1896.

Frederick's mother, Caroline was the daughter of Michael Searles, the architect known mainly for the Blackheath Paragon. Most of their children appeared to be adventurous, young Joseph and Robert were merchants who went to Australia. Robert returned to the UK and became a member of the Stock Exchange but Joseph with his wife and six children died in 1853 when the SS Madagascar, sailing from Melbourne to London with 110 passengers and a cargo that included gold dust, disappeared without trace. George also became a merchant, a rag merchant, and spent time in South Africa – at the same time and in the same area as Robert and Amelia Lungley. Frederick appeared to have the least adventurous life, following his father into the East India Company. By 1861 he is described as being retired (probably as a consequence of the Government taking over the administration of Indian affairs in 1858) and was staying with his brother George in Croydon.

Frederick and Emma Maitland had six children, Frederick Orbell, Edith Emma , Sophie Beatrice, Robert Lindley, Rhys and Eva Mary. Edith was born in Tenby and the rest in Croydon and Hampstead (where the family lived for the rest of their lives). In Hampstead the Maitlands were part of an artistic and politically active community and were Unitarians, worshipping at the Rosslyn Hill Chapel.

When the children grew up Emma Maitland left one of her daughters in charge of the family home at 18 Primrose Hill and embarked upon a prominent career in public life, particularly in female suffrage and education. However, she played little part in the suffragette movement, believing that the Woman's Suffrage Society was too antagonistic to men. She was a member of the executive of the Women's Local Government Society, a non-party feminist group established to promote the eligibility of women to serve on all local government bodies. She became President of the woman's branch of the Hampstead Liberal and Radical Association and represented it on the National Liberal Federation and the London Liberal and Radical Union. By 1890 she was vice-president of the Women's Liberal Federation. In 1888 Emma Maitland stood as a candidate for the London School Board, coming third in the list of the seven candidates elected to represent Marylebone, one of the ten divisions covering the whole of London.

DNB, Womans Penny Paper, Maitland Trust

Emma Maitland
Photograph from The Woman's
Penny Paper August 23rd 1890

  The Elementary Education Act of 1870 created elected school boards, which had power to build and run schools where there were insufficient voluntary school places; they could also compel attendance. Between 1870 and 1904, the London School Board was the single largest educational provider in London and the first directly elected body covering the whole of the Capital. Its electoral system contained several innovations, the board's election of 1870 was polled by secret ballot being the first large-scale election to use this approach in Britain, and women were permitted to vote and also to stand for election on the same terms as men.   Emma Maitland was displaced by a moderate faction in 1891 but was returned top of the poll for Chelsea in 1894 and held the seat until her retirement in 1904. She was elected by her peers to represent the London board on the Association of School Boards. Ironically, the success of the elected School Boards influenced the development of local government but the franchise of women ended with the Qualification of Women (County and Borough Councils) Act 1907. Emma Maitland played a key role in the campaign to keep women actively involved in the process and contributed to the provision that allowed their co-option, even if they were not franchised.

DNB, Womans Penny Paper, Maitland Trust

Turning to the children, Frederick junior went to sea, like his grandfather. By 1893 he had settled in Perth, Western Australia where he married Amy Glendon and farmed – the last reference that we find to him is in 1936, in Perth.

In 1883 Edith Maitland married David Sydney Waterlow, the son of MP, Lord Mayor of London and philanthropist, Sir Sydney Waterlow. David also entered parliament, as Liberal MP for North Hampstead between 1906 and 1910 but was mainly occupied in running the family printing and stationery business. They had five children, Clive, Mervyn, Margaret, Joan and Sylvia. The eldest, Clive Maitland Waterlow, was to become one of the UK's leading airship pioneers in early years of the 20th century. He was involved in the development of the first British Army airship, Nulli Secundus, in 1907 and died tragically in 1917. Wing Commander Waterlow was Commanding Officer of the Airship Training Wing when an airship being taken back to the hanger with a trainee pilot on board, lifted out of control, carrying Clive Waterlow and two others into the air at the end of a mooring rope; they fell to their deaths.

Clive Maitland Waterlow (1885-1917)

Maitland Trust, Natioal Archives, IGI, NLA, Australian Electoral Rolls, Sanger 2003

Sophie married Bryan Lee Leesmith, a lawyer, in 1893; they had a family but we cannot trace what happened to Sophie or her children. There is a letter on file written by "Bee Leesmith" in 1924 from Italy to David Waterlow. Robert Maitland became a civil engineer and went to Australia – possibly following Frederick – and married Ira Jenny. They had two daughters, Lorna and Enid Erica. Robert died in Port Said in 1912 and later that year the family trust was corresponding with Ira in Weisbaden about a settlement to provide for Lorna and Erica. The family returned to Perth where in 1936 Lorna was still living with Ira and described as a teacher. Rhys Maitland also tried Australia but returned to the UK to become a stockbroker. However, by 1904 his mother wrote that "*Rhys is no longer able to make a living on the Stock Exchange so is to go to the Transvaal to take up a farm under the scheme formulated by Lord Milner*". He died, as a farmer, in Kenya in 1925, leaving a widow, Edith.

In 1897, Eva married Ernest Aves, a social researcher. The Aves family, Eva, Ernest, Evangeline and Geraldine lived for a period at the beginning of the twentieth century at no 5 Lexden Terrace. Ernest Aves worked closely with Charles Booth on the inquiry into poverty in London: *Life and Labour of the People in London* published 1902/3 which was to have a profound influence on social policy. Their daughter Geraldine Maitland Aves, born 1898 and partly brought up in Tenby, was educated at Newnham College, Cambridge and worked for the London County Council. In 1941 she became Chief Welfare Officer at the Ministry of Health with particular responsibility for the evacuation of children. In 1945 she was seconded to the United Nations' Relief and Rehabilitation Administration as its Chief Child Care consultant in Europe before returning to Britain and the Home Office in 1946 to become the first head of a permanent welfare division and one of the key engineers of the post-war welfare system. Geraldine Aves retired in 1963 but remained active and prominent in the social welfare fields. In 1973 she founded The Volunteer Centre which collected and distributed information on volunteer recruitment and training at a national level, remaining its Vice-president from 1977 to the end of her life. She was made a Dame of the British Empire in 1977 but remained active in many fields of social welfare until she died in 1986.

Maitland Trust, Australian Electoral Rolls, National Archives, BMD, DNB.

John Rees wealth and investments had been placed in trust, initially for the benefit of his wife and subsequently for that of his daughter; this became known as "The Maitland Trust". In 1885 the Maitland Trust was brought before the High Court of Chancery to amend its terms. Thereafter, Emma Maitland started disposing of the Trust assets, the last disposal being Lexden Terrace which was sold piecemeal in 1922. In a letter dated 1919, Emma wrote to Henry Brown (a trustee) complaining of the low rents and high maintenance costs of Lexden Terrace; *"the war tax is the last straw…what can we get for it… would it make a good hotel? "*

Emma Maitland died at her home 43 Howitt Road Hampstead on 13 June 1923 aged 78. Frederick pre-deceased her, having died in 1902.

It had taken only two generations for the family to rise from that of a seaman in an out of the way resort in West Wales, to become part of the political elite in London. Emma Maitland and her family made a significant contribution to social welfare and, ultimately, to the emergence of the Welfare State. It is, perhaps, ironic that they were able to do so because of the family wealth, a legacy of the opium trade, a trade of which they did, no doubt, disapprove.

Appendix 1 Canton Petition, 24th December 1830

Source: **The Canton Register,** *Vol. III, 18 Dec. 1830, Issue No 25.*

To the Honourable the Commons of the United Kingdom of Great Britain and Ireland in Parliament Assembled.
The Humble Petition' of the Undersigned British Subjects in China

Humbly sheweth,

   That your petitioners having long submitted in silence to the oppressive and corrupt rule of the Chinese Government, consider it a duty alike owing to their country and to themselves to bring their grievances to the notice of your Honourable House, at this important crisis, when the regulation of British intercourse with China engages the attention of the legislature, in consequence of the approaching termination of the East India Company's charter.

         While British intercourse with other considerable states in the world is regulated by international treaties, that with the Chinese Empire is abandoned to the arbitrary control of the local authorities of Canton, a venal and corrupt class of persons, who having purchased their appointments, study only the means of amassing wealth by extortion and injustice, equally unrestrained by their own, and unopposed by the governments whose subjects they oppress. For the attainment of this end, severe burdens are imposed upon commerce, unsanctioned by, and frequently in defiance of, commands from the Imperial Government at Peking; to which the most erroneous reports are made of occurrences in this remote province, while no means of counteraction by opposing statements, are in any way afforded to your petitioners.

         From the earliest period of British subjects resorting to this Empire, trade has been the sole subject, a desire to promote which, and sometimes, (it must be admitted,) a nervous anxiety for its preservation, have subjected foreigners to privations and treatment to which it would be difficult to find a parallel in any part of the world. China was too remote from England, and the commerce was too limited to render it, in former years, a subject of much national interest; but during the whole course of the eighteenth, and still more during the present century, it has been gradually increasing, in defiance of Chinese restrictions, until it has reached a point of such important magnitude, as, your petitioners feel satisfied, will raise the anxiety of your Honourable House to place it, if it be possible, upon a permanent and honourable basis.

Your petitioners entertain the firm belief that much may be obtained from the fears, but that nothing will ever be conceded by the goodwill, of the Chinese government. In confirmation of this opinion the attention of your Honorable House need only be entreated to the total failure of both the Embassies to the Court of Peking in every respect, except the high principle which was maintained in the refusal to acquiesce in humiliating and degrading requisitions; which your petitioners are convinced produced a moral effect of the most beneficial tendency upon the minds of the Chinese. That these embassies were undertaken with a view to the improvement of the condition of British subjects in China, your petitioners are deeply sensible, and indeed find this expressed in the instructions from His Majesty's ministers to Lord Macartney. 'Under these circumstances it would become the dignity and character of His Majesty, to extend his paternal regard to these, his distant subjects, even if the commerce and prosperity of the nation were not concerned in their success, and to claim the Emperor of China's particular protection of them, with that weight which is due to the requisition of one great sovereign to another.' Your petitioners trust that His Majesty's government may ever be influenced by similar opinions. It is with considerable regret however that your petitioners make another brief extract from the same instructions, unhappily still descriptive of the condition in which they remain. Hitherto however Great Britain has been obliged to pursue the trade with that country, under circumstances the most discouraging, hazardous to its agents employed in conducting it and precarious to the various interests involved in it. The only place where His Majesty's subjects have the privilege of a factory is at Canton: the fair competition of the market is there destroyed by associations of the Chinese. Our supercargoes are denied open access to the tribunals of the country and to the equal execution of its laws, and are kept altogether in a most arbitrary state of depression, ill suited to the importance of the concerns which are entrusted to their care and scarcely compatible with the regulations of civilized society.'

The result of two British Embassies, in common with those of all other European governments, will forcibly suggest to your Honourable House how little is to be gained in China, by any of the refinements of diplomacy. The whole history of the foreign intercourse with this country demonstrates that a firm opposition to the arrogance and unreasonable pretensions of its government, even with imperfect means, has, sooner or later, been followed by an amicable and conciliatory disposition. While the Portuguese of Macao maintained this independence they were treated by the Chinese government with respect, and carried out an extensive and advantageous commerce, but when they adopted a servile course of policy, they were regarded with contempt, and a flourishing colony has gradually sunk into misery and decay. Even violence has frequently received friendly treatment at the hands of this Government, while obedience and conformity of the arbitrary laws, have met only with the return of severity and oppression. In the history of English commerce with China, many instances of this description exist. When Admiral Drury, in compliance with the reiterated commands of the Canton Government yielded up possession of Macao, which for several months had been garrisoned by a British force, the most contumelious and threatening proclamations were issued against him; and he was declared to have fled from a dread of the punishment which awaited him. About the same period, after a horde of pirates well-known by the name of 'Ladrones' had, for a succession of years, ravaged the southern coasts of the Empire, and committed numerous atrocities, their leader, a man of bold and determined character, was received in person by the Viceroy with every mark of respect, invested with a robe of honour, and ultimately nominated to an important official situation.

A British Admiral for his forbearance was despised and treated with indignity; the leader of pirates and banditti was, in reward of his atrocities, received with the most ceremonious attention, and was ranked among the nobility of the land. It is with no wish to advocate deeds of violence that these statements are made; but such is the people and such the Government of the Chinese Empire. This submissive spirit was exhibited in the most striking manner which can indicate the character of a nation when, at the last Tartar conquest this most ancient Empire of the world, containing so many millions of comparatively civilized human beings was subdued by its bitterest enemies, and yielded implicit obedience to a tribe of rude and ignorant barbarians.

Your petitioners earnestly entreat the consideration of your Honourable House to the fact, that the merciless and indiscriminating laws of China, as applied to foreigners, make no distinction between manslaughter and murder. In those cases (happily few) of the death of a native by the hand of a foreigner, the life of an individual of the same nation (it being immaterial whether the offender or not) is invariably demanded, without reference to the palliating circumstances recognized by Chinese law, as modifying the offence and its punishment, where natives alone are concerned. On all such occasions the Chief of the nation, supposed to be implicated, is required to find out the guilty person, to point out his name and deliver him up, that the local magistrate may try and punish him, which having been proved by melancholy experience to mean nothing else than summary execution, he is in fact required to select and surrender a victim for strangulation, to appease the sanguinary malice of this Government. Such a requisition admits of but one reply, since no foreigners in China have authority from their own governments to judge or deliver up even a guilty fellow subject: and, on the other hand, non-compliance is sure to be followed by a total suspension of trade with the nation concerned. The necessity of thus permitting the guilty to escape, in order to secure the safety of the innocent, is an evil deeply to be lamented, and loudly calling for the interposition of your Honourable House. It is much to the honour of the British Factory that, since the year 1784, when an innocent man was seized and executed by the Government of Canton, a firm and effectual resistance has been made against the enforcement of this unjust requisition, though such resistance has invariably given rise to suspension of commercial intercourse, and long protracted discussions with the Government.

While your petitioners acknowledge it is an undeniable principle, that foreigners should yield obedience to the law of the country in which they reside they submit that this doctrine cannot be maintained in favour of a government which like the Chinese, withholds from foreigners the protection of its laws. And whose power is felt only in a system of unceasing oppression pursued on the avowed principle of considering every people as placed many degrees below its own in the scale of human beings.

Your petitioners will now briefly advert to some of the principal commercial disabilities to which they are subjected. English ships were formerly admitted to trade at various ports; Amoy, Ningpo, and the islands of Chusan and Fonmosa but of late, the entire foreign commerce of this vast Empire has been restricted to the single port of Canton, where the exorbitant harbour dues operate as a virtual exclusion of the smaller class of shipping while the privilege of dealing with foreigners is confined to some ten or twelve licensed native merchants, such is the oppressive conduct of the local authorities towards these individuals by a systematic course of constantly recurring exactions and generally harsh treatment that respectable and wealthy men cannot be prevailed on to accept the privilege though earnestly urged by the Government to do so, for the purpose of suppluing vacancies arising from death and bankruptcies. The Government being thus unable to maintain, in an efficient state, the limited medium of intercourse they have established, and prohibiting foreigners from renting warehouses in which to deposit their cargoes, there is no adequate competition, nor any chance of obtaining a fair market value of a commodity; an evil the more deeply felt in consequence of nearly all imports for the year necessarily arriving about the same time, during the few months when the periodical winds are favourable in the China sea. From the moment a foreign vessel arrives, her business is liable to be delayed by the underlings of the Customs house, on frivolous pretexts for the sake of extorting unauthorized charges — the duty on her import cargo is levied in an arbitrary manner by low unprincipled men, who openly demand bribes – it is consequently of uncertain amount, and, by the addition of local exactions exceeds by many times, the rates, prescribed by the Imperial Tariff, which appear to be in general, moderate, although so little attended to in practice, that it is scarcely possible to name any fixed charge except on a very few articles.

It is unnecessary to occupy the time of your Honourable House, by dwelling on the individual and national loss arising from this oppressive and corrupt system. It would be equally out of place to enter into a detail of the many studied indignities heaped upon foreigners by acts of this Government, and by the contumelious edicts placarded on the walls of their very houses, representing them as addicted to the most revolting crimes, with no other object than to stamp them in the eyes of the people as a barbarous, ignorant, and depraved race, everyway inferior to themselves, thereby exciting the lower orders to treat them with habitual insolence.

Suffice it to say that no privation or discomfort, is too minute to escape notice, in the pursuit of this ever present purpose. Free air and exercise are curtailed, by precluding access to the country, or beyond the confined streets in the immediate vicinity of their habitations. Even the sacred ties of domestic life are disregarded, in the separation of husband and wife, parent and child, regarded unavoidable by a capricious prohibition of foreign ladies residing in Canton, for which there appears to be no known law, and not other authority than the plea of usage.

Your petitioners consider it a duty which they owe to truth and justice to declare to your Honourable House, that they attribute the evils which have been enumerated to the nature and character of the Chinese Government, and not to any want of proper spirit and firmness in the Agents of the East India Company, who have on various occasions opposed effectual resistance to many of them, which could not have been attempted by individuals pursuing their separate interests, and unconnected by any bond of union. The servants of the Company have insisted on being heard by the Government, and have maintained the right of addressing it in the Chinese language, when that has been denied to other foreigners. Privileges have thus been repeatedly gained, and the most serious evils averted.

The influence which the East India Company has acquired by its extensive dealings, furnishes the strongest evidence of the importance of foreign commerce to this self sufficient people. Your petitioners are however of opinion that, to place the commercial interests of Great Britain on that fair and equitable footing to which they are entitled, a higher authority is required, emanating directly from His Majesty, as a medium of communication with the Canton Government as well as with the Imperial Court at Peking; which would remove the impression prevalent among the Chinese authorities, that foreigners in China have forfeited the protection of their own sovereigns, as in the case with natives of China who leave this country. Your petitioners would anticipate the most beneficial results from the permanent residence at Peking of a representative of His Majesty instructed to act with becoming spirit in protecting the interests of his countrymen; an arrangement which, they believe, was considered of such importance as to be one of the principal objects of the last Embassy. And as the Russians, who conduct the trade on the frontiers between that Empire and China, have long had the privilege of resorting to Peking, to acquire the language in a college expressly established for the purpose, it is reasonable to suppose that the residence of British subjects would, if insisted on, be also tolerated, more particularly as they would no longer have to contend with the religious and political jealousy of the Roman Catholic Missionaries formerly established at Peking but now dismissed.

The successful termination of the Burmese war and the approximation of British dominion in India to the confines of China are well known in this country, and a remonstrance from the British Government would, your petitioners have reason to believe, be received with a deference and attention never yet accorded to any Embassy, all of which have been conducted on the erroneous principle of attempting to negotiate for that which, if firmly demanded, could not have been withheld, while the Ambassadors have been designated 'Tribute bearer' and recognized in no other light than that of public officers deputed by inferiors Princes to offer presents and acknowledge vassalage to the supreme Sovereign of the earth. But your petitioners cannot deny to the Chinese Government the credit of having hitherto successfully triumphed over European power and dignity. The ruler of the most ancient Empire has seen the representatives of the Monarchs of other countries bear tribute to his throne, and, in many instances, prostrate themselves in the dust before him, while he has treated their abject and subservient spirit with the general indifference which it deserved.

Unless through the direct intervention of His Majesty's Government, in communication with the Court at Peking, your petitioners fear that no material extension of British commerce, or effectual amelioration of the humiliating conditions of British subjects, in China, can be expected. If unattainable by the course suggested your petitioners indulge a hope that the Government of Great Britain with the sanction of the legislature, will adopt a resolution worthy of the nation and by the acquisition of an insular possession near the coast of China place British commerce, in this remote quarter of the globe, beyond the reach of future despotism and oppression.

Your petitioners therefore humbly pray that your Honourable House will take the premises into your consideration and grant such relief as to our wisdom may appear expedient.

And your petitioners will ever pray, &c.

CANTON, CHINA, 24th December, 1830   *Le Pichon 2006*

Appendix 2   Notes on Lexden Terrace

Lexden Terrace is the only physical memorial that we have to John Rees. Grade 2* listed and described variously as Tenby's finest terrace and Tenby's finest nineteenth century houses, Lexden Terrace is both interesting in its own right and interesting because of some of the people who have been associated with it.

John Smith, the builder.

John Smith was the most prominent builder in Tenby at the time, part of a family which was commissioned by the Corporation to undertake building work as far back as the seventeenth century and included Ambrose who had built much of Georgian Tenby. The Smiths were very active in the building trade and there are no fewer than three John Smiths born about the turn of the 19th century – John the carpenter in South Parade, John the mason in St Julian Street and John the builder – so there is much room for confusion. John the builder was born in 1801 so a contemporary of John Rees, and lived in Quay Hill. In addition to building, he is described as a maltster and publican; for many years, John Smith ran the *Wheatsheaf,* now called *The Lifeboat Tavern.* A memoir in the Tenby Observer (1st October 1906) said: *"Mr Smith was a little man, always dressed in trousers of yellow cord, tailcoat and waistcoat with bright buttons, and a broad brimmed beaver hat. Many of the most prominent tradesmen met in his parlour where business deals were carried out and yarns spun, helped by the finest home-brewed, and strong tobacco smoked in long Churchwarden pipes".* John Smith, until his death at the age of 93, lived in Quay Street. He installed a fanlight over his door identical to those that he had installed at Lexden Terrace – this is still there, opposite Plantagenet House.

National Archives, Tenby Observer.

Tour of the houses

Clues to the original layout and use can be found in the tradesmen's bills, a 1855 inventory on John Rees' death, the 1862 sale catalogue of the furnishings of no1 and a dilapidations schedule of 1876, plus certain features still intact of the houses themselves.

The vaulted entrance hall gives access to a room with gothic traceried windows designated as 'the library'; in the original design this probably opened from the staircase hall. The staircase hall beyond is separated by double doors (these are unlikely to part of the original design, the triumph of Victorian privacy over Regency ostentation) and is dominated by a curved cantilevered staircase terminating at the base in a Greek revival newel-post. The staircase is top lit by a circular lantern with daintily curved plasterwork leading into it. Beyond is the dining room which was typically masculine with a fireplace surround of local black 'snowdrop' marble and black japanned door furniture and bell levers (from Hindley and Son in Oxford Street), allowing access through floor length sash windows to the terrace (in a 1872 note, the cupboard in the dining room was rather quaintly referred to as a "*Ladies Pantry*"). On the first floor the drawing room has a white marble fireplace surround (also probably local), cream ceramic fittings and access through floor length sash windows to a balcony with ornamental cast balustrading and a zinc curved canopy painted in stripes. The houses are described as having three bedrooms. There is reference to a dressing room, presumably the location of the present second floor bathroom – but this may have resulted from a later division of a bedroom.

There are, of course, the attic rooms, the kitchen and the housekeeper's room (this contains a cupboard with substantial brick and slate shelving – possibly a wine store). Other references are to the butler's pantry (the basement room under the stairs), the scullery and the larder (the rear cellars). The front cellar contained coals and the servants' closet. The room off the staircase between the first and second floors, with a curved door and gothic lights, is described as a WC. The woodwork in the principal rooms was grained in either satinwood or birds eye maple and the walls papered mainly with floral wallpapers. All of the south-east facing windows had sliding venetian shutters (to protect the delicate and costly crown glass from hail and storms) and wire fly screens. *Girouard 1990. Maitland Trust, Rees Papers, Brunswick, Lloyd 2004.*

The external woodwork was oak grained and the street doors *"any colour as Mr Rees decides".* The walls were painted in stone colour. The colour of the ironwork is described as "to harmonise with the wall colour" and would probably have been bronze green. Externally, the terrace at the rear would have been a continuous promenade, with steps at each end. Steps outside No.5 would have led to a path within the boundary wall and steps outside No.1 under an archway in the wall towards the beach. At the front, a carriage drive went round a triangular bed, probably planted with roses (a list of varieties is given in an invoice from Garaway Mayes of Bristol). The front of the houses was unencumbered with the ugly drainage pipes which disfigure them today; there was no mains drainage necessitating the soil pipes and internal evidence shows that the rainwater was routed from the front guttering to an internal drain. The rainwater from the rear was routed into a large slate cistern in the cellar. It also appears that there was a fenced or walled place at the front where rubbish could be deposited for collection in the corner opposite no 5. The giant ionic pilasters above a string course at the front are a little crude of execution and one wonders whether later re-rendering has obscured details; it has certainly covered the recesses for the doorbells and foot scrapers. The views from the back are magnificent but at the time of building there would also have been better views from the front; the buildings opposite in St Julian's Street which are presently two storied were single storied in 1843. The roof structure is unusual, being six pitch and although we can find this feature in detached and semi-detached villas, we can find no other example of it in terraced housing.

Samuel Burleigh Gabriel

As noted in the main text, one candidate for the preparation of building drawings would be the Clifton architect S. B. Gabriel. On 22 September 1845 John Rees made out a cheque for £2.9.0 to him and described him on the stub as "architect". Although this is late in terms of the construction and the sum is modest, it demonstrates a relationship that could go back to when they were neighbours in Clifton. Samuel Burleigh Gabriel was born in Clifton in 1827/8 and went into partnership with John Hicks of Dorchester (better known as the first employer of the author Thomas Hardy). The "Burleigh" in his name refers to an Indian connection and Gabriel's younger sister Dorothy married Rees' associate, Charles Gutzlaff.

Maitland Trust, Birt, Rees Papers, Muthesius 1982

Lexden House

The house now known as Lexden House was built between 1844 and 1850 by Rachel Williams as 6 Lexden Terrace in order to exploit the letting potential of John Rees' new development next door. It was constructed on the property of the Williams family which immediately adjoined that of John Rees. Rachel Williams agreed in 1844 to lease from her sisters and her brother their share of the family house which she demolished, before building an additional house on the end of Lexden Terrace. The new house was complete by the time Rachel Williams drew up her will in April 1850. She died in June 1850 leaving all to her sister, Bridget Reynolds Williams, who thus owned No.6 excepting a residual interest that remained with her brother, John Jackson Williams. Bridget continued to live in St Mary Street, letting No.6 for holiday use. Charles Smith, a wealthy mine-owner from Llansamlet, bought the house in 1867; he had been Sheriff of Glamorgan and Mayor of Swansea, later becoming Mayor of Tenby. He renamed No.6 as Lexden House, setting about a programme of improvements. Chief amongst these was the purchase of the house adjoining which he demolished, thus creating improved access and an improved aspect to his own house, and also gaining a substantial garden at the side. The house demolished by Smith may have been, or incorporated the *Nelson Tavern*, described as "*a small one story building .....where Dr Bryant's engine house now stands*". Dr Bryant bought the house in 1900 and it stayed in his family until the present owner purchased in 1991.

Some Residents

The other family which resided in Lexden Terrace for a lengthy period, nearly 80 years, was the Cravens of Bradford. As soon as the Maitlands expressed the intention of leaving Tenby, Joseph Craven, a worsted mill owner who had been advised to winter in a healthier climate, expressed interest in No.1. He was the main purchaser when the contents were auctioned and, on 15 February 1862, he signed a three year lease at £55 a year, taking out a 21 year lease in 1864. Craven was one of the principal benefactors of the Independent Church at the Old Tabernacle (now St John's), and is said to have had a fine art collection. In 1884, his sons, Frederick and Arthur Craven of Waterloo Mills took a lease for a further 21 years, mainly, it would seem, to use the house as a family holiday home, and when it was offered for sale in 1922, Frederick bought it for £900.

Maitland Trust, Johnson 2003, Hordley, St Davids, Hutton, Tenby Observer.

The Craven family sold No.1 to Geraldine Lawrence in 1939. She was a society hostess based in Chelsea with strong artistic connections and leanings. She used No.1 as her holiday house and also owned Little Rock House (one of the Greville houses) , next door but one, which she used for additional guest accommodation. Her guests at the time constituted much of the artistic life of London; they were entertained there and played on the beach and the pleasure ground. They included Laurie Lee, the novelist and poet, Anthony Devas, the painter and his wife, Nicolette Macnamara, her sister Caitlin Thomas (Dylan's wife) and the artist Norman Hepple.

Another literary connection was Cecil Woodham-Smith described in The Times 17 March 1977 as *"one of the most gifted biographers and narrative historians of her generation"* She was the daughter of James Fitzgerald, a retired Colonel in the Indian Army and formerly Deputy Commissioner for Berar in India, and his wife, Blanche Phillips of Picton Castle, Fitzgerald had been the tenant of No.2 in 1890.

A further artistic connection was Nina Hamnett, who was born in No.3 in 1890 and spent much of her early life there. Her grandfather, Wlliam Archdeacon,a leading naval cartographer, rented the house at £50 per annum in 1886. In 1891 he was living there with wife, daughter, son-in law (GE Hamnett, an army captain), grand-daughter (Nina); another naval staff commander and his wife were visiting and they had two servants and a nursemaid. Archdeacon died and was buried in Tenby. Nina Hamnett was a gifted artist who died in 1956 after a career as the legendary queen of bohemia in London and Paris. Her circle included Sickert, Wyndham Lewis, the Sitwells, and the Bloomsbury Group. She was a close friend of Modigliani and had affairs with Gaudier-Brzeska and Roger Fry. Her work is in the National Portrait Gallery and the Tenby Museum.

Two of the most famous Tenby artists were Augustus and Gwen John. Augustus was an enthusiastic follower of Robert Prust who lived at No.2 with his parents, three sisters, four servants and a parrot. Prust was the leader of the "Red Indian" tribe that ranged over the Burrows until its members (except Augustus) became bored – but even Augustus became disillusioned when Prust lost his nerve after the two of them had started a fire in a wood.

Hamnett 1932, Holroyd, 1974, National Archives.

The John's father, Edwin, himself moved to No.5 Lexden Terrace shortly after his family left Tenby. Gwen went to live in France and never returned to Tenby but Augustus was a visitor and, as a result of his father's will, briefly, in 1938, a part owner of No.5. When the houses were sold by the Maitlands in 1922, Edwin John purchased the house in which he lived and took responsibility for the common areas, including the forecourt.

There was at least one hero. In 1885 Francis Girardot signed the lease of No.2 for 3½ years at £50 a year. He was the originator of the saying *"Women and children first"*, known as "The Birkenhead Drill". Girardot had been a Lieutenant commanding a detachment of the 43rd Light Infantry on board HM Troopship Birkenhead, carrying reinforcements for the troops engaged in the Kaffir War. On 26th February 1852 the vessel suddenly struck a sunken rock with such force that within 20 minutes she was a wreck. Captain Wright reported *"When the vessel was just about going down the Commander called out, 'All those that can swim jump overboard and make for the boats!' Lieutenant Girardot and myself were standing on the stern part of the poop. We begged the men not to do as the Commander said as the boat with the women must be swamped. Not more than three made the attempt"*. All the women and children on board, 20 in number, were saved; 23 officers and 468 soldiers and sailors were drowned. About 170 men, including Girardot managed to get ashore, mainly by supporting themselves on driftwood.

By the end of the nineteenth century the Georgian style of house was unfashionable and regarded as being very inconvenient. Lexden Terrace slipped down the social scale and in the second half of the twentieth century, some of the houses were converted for multiple occupation. By the end of the Century, however,all were again in single family occupation and with a group of owners determined to restore them to their former standing. There has been substantial investment with some of the external work grant supported by the National Park and CADW. The Terrace is now in good order and a frequent backdrop for period dramas such as The Count of Monte Cristo, Vanity Fair and The Edge of Love.

Addison 1906

Appendix 3   Family Trees

The Rees Family of Tenby

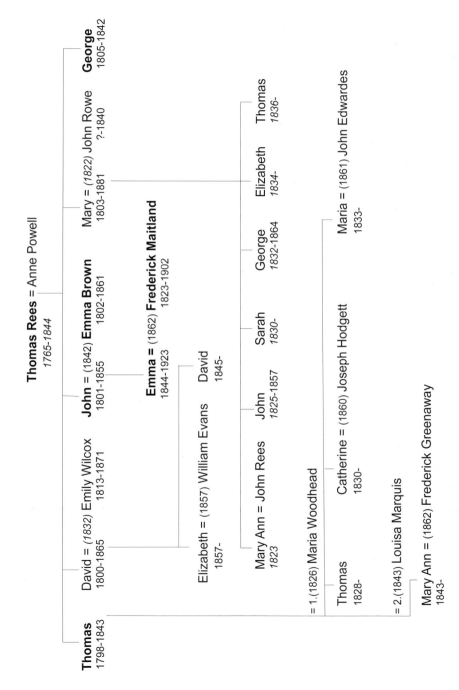

Principal characters are in bold. Estimated dates are in italics.

The Maitland Family of London

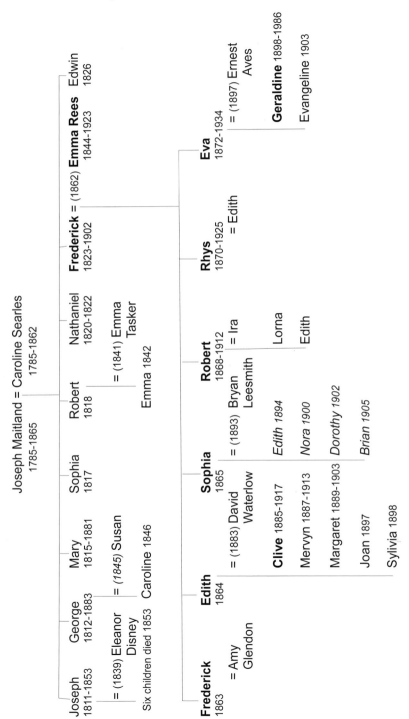

Joseph Maitland = Caroline Searles
1785-1865   1785-1862

- Joseph 1811-1853 = (1839) Eleanor Disney — Six children died 1853
- George 1812-1883 = (1845) Susan — Caroline 1846
- Mary 1815-1881
- Sophia 1817
- Robert 1818 = (1841) Emma Tasker — Emma 1842
- Nathaniel 1820-1822
- Frederick 1823-1902 = (1862) Emma Rees 1844-1923
- Edwin 1826

Frederick = Emma Rees children:

- Frederick 1863 = Amy Glendon
- Edith 1864 = (1883) David Waterlow
  - Clive 1885-1917
  - Mervyn 1887-1913
  - Margaret 1889-1903
  - Joan 1897
  - Sylivia 1898
- Sophia 1865 = (1893) Bryan Leesmith
  - Edith 1894
  - Nora 1900
  - Dorothy 1902
  - Brian 1905
- Robert 1868-1912 = Ira
  - Lorna
- Rhys 1870-1925 = Edith
  - Edith
- Eva 1872-1934 = (1897) Ernest Aves
  - Geraldine 1898-1986
  - Evangeline 1903

Principal characters are shown in bold. Unconfirmed information is shown in italics.

The Brown Family of Lexden

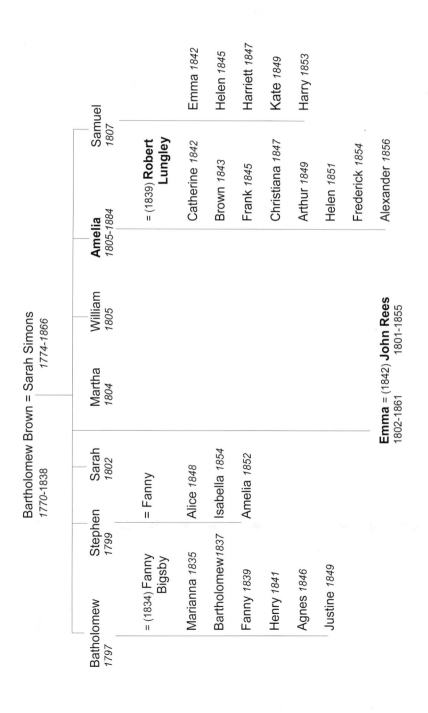

Sources, Bibliography and Acknowledgements

There are many excellent books on China Trade and the Opium Wars, the ones that we have used in compiling this account being listed below. Sources used in putting together the main text are indicated as footnotes and listed alphabetically.

Addison & Matthews, *Deathless Story of The Birkenhead and its heroes — a full account of the Birkenhead disaster.* Hutchinson & Co,1906.

Australian Electoral Rolls *are available on a number of websites including that of Ancestry.co.uk.*

Aves, Geraldine. *Papers of Geraldine Aves, 1908-1990* The Women's Library, part of London Metropolitan University.

Beeching, Jack, *The Chinese Opium Wars* Harcourt Brace Jovanovich 1975.

Birt, Charles Ltd. *1849 Illustrated Map of Tenby on display in the Office.*

BMD – *Birth Marriage and Death Registers,* General Register Office.

British Library - *Report of Hugh Hamilton Lindsey, Charts drawn by both Thomas and John Rees and genealogical information drawn from the India Office Records. The Newspaper Archives are also an invaluable source of the contemporary view of events.*

Brunswick Town Charitable Trust, *The Regency Town House.*

Canton Register. *The Canon Register started in 1827 by James and Alexander Matheson is an invaluable source of information for the period. In this research it has not proved practicable to obtain sight of the original and secondary sources have been used including Roger Houghton and his website "History 1793-1843".*

Collis, Maurice, *Foreign Mud, An Account of the Opium War:* Faber 1946.

Dalrymple Hay, Admiral Sir John, *The Suppression of Piracy in the China Sea, 1849.* Edward Stanford, London 1889.

De Quincy, Thomas, *Confessions of an Opium-Eater* Collins 1926.

DNB*, Oxford Dictionary of National Biography,* Oxford University Press 2004; article by Jane Martin on Emma Maitland.

Electoral Registers. *Registers for Tenby can variously be found in the Tenby Museum, the Pembrokeshire Record Office and the Haverfordwest Public Library.*

FIBIS, *The Families in British India Society (www.fibis.org) is an invaluable source of information on people who have lived and worked in India and China.*

Galvin Tony, *Sea of Change*; Gaffer 2002.

Girouard, Mark, *The English Town;* Yale University press 1990.

Godsall, Jon R, *The Tangled Web: A Life of Sir Richard Burton*; Troubador Publishing Ltd, 2008.

Grace, Professor Richard, Providence College, Rhode Island. *Paper to the 2006 Conference of the Boston Historical Society.*

Greenberg, Michael, *British Trade and the Opening of China 1800-1842* ; CUP 1951.

Greville , Charles, *Memoirs*. Appleton and Company, New York 1875.

Gutzlaff, Charles, *Journal of three voyages along the coast of China in 1831, 1832, & 1833*. Frederick Westley and A. H. Davis, 1834.

Hague, William, *William Wilberforce*. Harper 2008.

Hamnett, Nina. *Laughing Torso* fp1932; Kessinger Publishing 2004.

Holroyd, Michael, *Augustus John*; Heinemann 1974.

Hordley T. W., *Reminiscences of Tenby 1854-1934* (privately published)

Howard, Joseph Jackson and Frederick Arthur Crisp, *Visitation of England and Wales* privately printed in 1896 and "republished" on-line by Google.

Hunter, William C, *An American in Canton;* Journal of the Royal Asiatic Society 1966.

Hutton, Marion, *Lexden House conveyances*.

IGI, *International Genealogical Index*, Church of the Latter Day Saints.

India Office, *biographical information on people who served and lived in India.*

JM Archive *Jardine Matheson Archive in Cambridge University. The full archive is extensive and has been used as a source for several of the books quoted, the index and brief description of the contents (available on the Cambridge University Janus website) can also be helpful in locating individuals.*

Johnson, Keith*, The Pubs of Pembroke etc :* Logaston Press 2003.

Le Pichon, Alain, *China Trade and Empire: Jardine, Matheson & Co. and the Origins of British Rule in Hong Kong*; Oxford University Press, 2006 *Probably the most useful of the "Chinese" source documents in that a great deal of the correspondence between Jardine and Matheson from the archive is quoted verbatim.*

Lloyd, Orbach, Scourfield, *The Buildings of Wales - Pembrokeshire;* Yale University Press 2004.

LSE - London School of Economics, *Charles Booth On-Line Archive.*

Maitland Trust Papers D/EE/17 – Pembrokeshire County Record Office. *This is a very extensive set of documents relating to the management of the property left by John Rees, mainly between 1855 and 1922, deposited by Eaton Evans, the successors to Evans, Powell and Matthias.*

Merrony, Mark W., *An Official History of Tenby;* Merrony 2004.

Miles, Dillwyn, *Lieutenant John George Letters 1799-1808*; Gwasg Dinefwr Press 2002

Muthesius, Stephen, *The English Terraced House* ; Yale University Press 1982.

Napier, Priscilla, *Barbarian Eye, Lord Napier in China 1834* ; Brassey's 1995.

National Archives, *An invaluable source of data. Principally used in this account are Census returns, available at ten year intervals from 1841 to 1911, and copies of wills presented for probate at Canterbury, in particular those of John and Thomas Rees.*

NLA - National Library of Australia, *– copies of the Melbourne Argus and other old Australian newspapers are available on the web-site, http://ndpbeta.nla.gov.au.*

Pembrokeshire Herald, *Microfilm copies are available in the Pembrokeshire County Library at Haverfordwest.*

Pettigrew, Jane, *Design for Tea;* Sutton Publishing 2003.

Pottinger, George, *Sir Henry Pottinger, First Governor of Hong Kong*; Sutton Publishing 1997.

Price, Brian*, Two Tenby Duels;* Journal of Pembrokeshire Historical Society No 15 2006 *plus additional research undertaken into the East India Company papers in the British Library.*

Rees Papers D/EE/55 – Pembrokeshire Record Office. *These are miscellaneous papers relating to various of John Rees' business interests.*

Ride, Lindsay and May, *An East India Company Cemetery*; Protestant Burials in Macao, Ed Bernard Mellor; Hong Kong University Press 1995.

Rose, Richard, *Pembroke People* Otterquill Books 2000.

St David's - *Wills Proved* – Pembrokeshire Record Office.

St Mary's Church Tenby, *Parish Register and List of Monumental Inscriptions* – Pembrokeshire Record Office.

Sanger, Ray. *Clive Maitland Waterlow*: Cross and Cockade vol 34 no 4 2003; First World War Aviation Historical Society.

Swansea Library. *Cambrian Newspaper Archive. On-line resource.*

Suggett, Richard. *John Nash Architect in Wales*; National Library of Wales 1995.

Sutton, Jean, *Lords of the East; The East India Company and Its Ships*: Conway Maritime Press, 1981.

The Tablet; May 16 1840.

Tenby Museum and Art Gallery, *Various deeds and maps in the Tenby Museum and Art Gallery, including a schedule to the Lock papers, Electoral Registers, extracts of the St Mary's Register and extracts from the Tenby Council Minutes.*

Tenby Observer and Visitors List. *Local newspaper including a list of visitors commencing in 1853. Also 8/2/1957 Article by "Old Tenbyite" Copies are available for research at the Newspaper Offices in Tenby.*

Thompson F.M.L., *English Landed Society in the Nineteenth Century* – Routledge & Keegan Paul 1963.

Tipton, John, *Fair and Fashionable Tenby;* Tenby Museum and Art Gallery 1987.

Times Newspaper Archive.

Welsh Mariners.co.uk. *A helpful website built up by Dr Reg Davies with biographical information on some 24,000 individuals.*

Waley, Arthur,*The Opium War Through Chinese Eyes;* George Allen & Unwin 1958.

Walker, Richard. *A former owner of No.1 Lexden Terrace was generous with information and with access to original deeds.*

Warrane Lecture *given by the Chief Justice of New South Wales, Sydney, 20 September 2006.*

Women's Penny Paper August 23rd 1860 *Interview with Emma Maitland.*

Wylie, Alexander, *Memorials of Protestant Missionaries to the Chinese*; American Presbyterian Mission Press, 1867.

Victoria County Histories in www.british-history.ac.uk.

Photographs and details of Emma Rees' resting place were provided by Leonard Rees. Photograph of George Rees' grave and reference to his death notice provided by Ena Niedergang. The cover illustration is an original picture by Naomi Tidemann.

Particular thanks must be given to the staff of the Pembrokeshire Record Office, the Tenby County Library and of the Tenby Museum and Art Gallery who have been most supportive Neighbours and Tenby residents have also given access to material and Marion Hutton of Lexden House has been especially helpful. However, the greatest thanks are due to my patient and assiduous research assistant, my wife, Elizabeth.

Index